THE HORSES

THE HORSES
New & Selected Poems

by

Richard Silberg

RED HEN PRESS | *Pasadena, CA*

The Horses: New & Selected Poems

Book design and layout by Ina Jungmann

Library of Congress Cataloging-in-Publication Data

Silberg, Richard, 1942 –
    The horses : new & selected poems : poems / by Richard Silberg.—1st ed.
        p. cm.
    ISBN 978-1-59709-231-9
    I. Title.
    PS3569.I4145H67 2012
    813'.54—dc23

                                2012006928

The National Endowment for the Arts, the Los Angeles County Arts
Commission, the Ahmanson Foundation, the Los Angeles Department of
Cultural Affairs, and the James Irvine Foundation partially support Red
Hen Press.

First Edition
Published by Red Hen Press
www.redhen.org

ACKNOWLEDGMENTS

Grateful acknowledgment is made to the following journals in which some of these poems first appeared.

The Addison Street Anthology: Berkeley's Poetry Walk, edited by Robert Hass and Jessica Fisher, "The Audience"; *American Poetry Review*, "The Crows," "The Fields," "For Poetry"; *The Berkeley Poetry Review*, "The Golden Gate"; *Denver Quarterly*, "Poetizing at the Med"; *Eleven Eleven*, "Godfighter"; *OntheBus*, "Door"; *New American Writing*, "Dog's Eye"; *Parthenon West Review*, "Moving," "Tantrum"; *Paterson Literary Review*, "Steering the Train," "The Page"; *VOLT*, "The Ache"; *ZYZZYVA*, "So to Speak."

Contents

FROM **TOTEM POLE** (1996)

FROM **DOUBLENESS** (2000)

THE HORSES

FROM

TRANSLUCENT GEARS

1982

A Song for the Piano Player

Sleazing in a basement
   in Northern California
I hear the black kids
hoot from Harlem
horn fisted graceful
as scary sugar

My Daddy comes
to me moping
a pack rat
torn sheet and rubber mat
in my teen-age thirties
a writer living in bare places

Daddy be my juju
be my African black sceptre
give me courage Daddy
that I be strong
when I face the lion

Down in the black
   ocean streets
I fought psychopathic
cross-wise Sanford
and when his fist
exploded in my head

it was my mother's rage
that rose in me
   and won

Was that the lion
the dragon of my passage?
    or is he here
in this damp winter basement
spiders weaving on the walls
    breathing here
in this gray scuzzy flow
of places
and faces without roots
or flowers
the dragon of failure
of middle age and death?

I hated you then, Daddy
I was ashamed
when I needed someone
to show me how to be a man

We played games instead
    you and I
together like two little boys
travelling on the lit up nerves
    of Manhattan

to Hopalong Cassidy movies
    on Saturdays in Times Square
to the Museum of Natural History
    the Bronx Zoo

You told me stories
shaving in the mornings
about Oscar Schmulewitz
    and his Daddy
their wondrous adventures
travelling by helicopter to Africa
    being swallowed by whales

My slight funny Daddy
cared for by women

A juju for the hollowness
    the concrete and the strangers
a chieftain's amulet and scars
to brave this shapeless river
    of our lives
where we struggle
like little fishes

It's all different now
    an undreamt land
of strange golden hills
swelling like breasts
mountains to the north
ocean to the west

No collapsing black star
    of New York island
fabulous auras
of show business greats

you booked in the Catskills
　　when they were little
of ex-champs
blinking in the Broadway lights
who called you 'Commodore'
and taught me
how to hold my dukes

　　no strutting shadows
only bland healthy faces
the wild popcorn boys
I fought in the schoolyard
are junkies or night porters
　　squashed candy wrappers
that flutter on other streets

A charm Daddy
a magician's light
to unclench my fists
so the sap can flow
to the middle of my life
so I can stand
in wide horizontal spaces
and listen to the earth

　　before my birth
you were a young man
piano player on the road
　　I hear you playing
BOOM-CHICK BOOM-CHICK

funny Al
   slick
in lonely towns
Dallas, Rio de Janeiro
making up songs
   for the waitresses

Who you are
a basic party harlequin
only your sensitivity your nervousness
slight clever build
   quick
a woman's man
   runner
and a lover
not a fighter

The nervous center
that you couldn't share with anyone
not with Mother or with me
          sealed off
in punchlines and babytalk
golf TV laughter
   hard timeless nut of you
dangling inside your seventy years
moustachio moon face and jowls
round belly skinny legs

   gleaming soul nut
unravelling to drop
so soon

I'll store it for my winter
the juju of my father
    sunlight before birth
      the channel
juju of the nervous funny
      talking man
Who I am
conjuring here
in the basement

A nervous funny
talking man
with courage
from my mother

a golden oval
   juju

to let my Daddy go
to feel the cats
the rhythm flow
the black girls
dancing in a row
Marilyn and Sonya
molasses and honey

And when the whale comes
to swallow me
in the ocean, Daddy
to know who I am

THE AUDITION

This cat jumps up to my table
   an actor he says
   out of our sly past
running around each other
in and out of pastel doors

a black cat
serpentine
lithe obsidian blade

     mumble mumble
    auditions
    mumble seven hundred bucks
    from his old lady
    Hollywood mumble
    talent and beauty

the round conviction of his face
circles galaxies of want
resplendent thrones
caged white leopards

I want you to come out
and listen to this speech
    Othello

   in the park
   he readies himself
   becomes
   a planted broomstick

children play behind his head
   while he declaims
   down a long murky hall

sunlight searching in the grass
needles into
blue-veined tiny flowers
with dark blue
smoky threads of pollen

He has beauty too
honey light in his darkness
curved as Nefertiti
on the prow of her ship of Afterlife
curved frozen black beauty

   waiting in his sunlit hallway
for the turbaned moor
who will never appear

   money
   stardom

for the pig of light to come rooting at his soul

TALL BLOSSOM

I was
bellowing
in the shadows
of a vast cathedral

when you came stoking along
        on cool stilts
like an old cut
from the Coasters

Your long silver head
        possessed itself
churning it out
in starry slow motion

hit a penny
hit a penny
      bump a nickle twice
bump it jellybean nice

eyes of a newborn baby
dark steel blue
receding to
chalk cliffs and the sea
a little horse in California
        prison time

I love you
   I love you   I said

tall silver blossom
ultra-Rilkean beebop angel

No time
no time   you said
I'm a bruised blues singer
   light and gay
I've acted in England
and danced ballet

No time
no time
See how the leopard
   eats my flesh
I'm a little shorn lamb
birds sing
   in my hair

Then I knew who you were
alone
flowering
between the sea and the sky
brilliant heads
   of our lovelessness

my painful sister
dancing
in the vast cathedral

DESERT

You've got to
        keep coming
on the other hand
there's the black glove
casual
      Botticelli placed
over the cunt

reclining in a train robbery
in cactus country

on the other hand
the poem of your funkiness
and wrinkles
your shopworn beautiful speed trip

fast as an antelope, McClellan!

men and women slam out
180° bad
in Berkeley-Oakland
     it's like
people are murdering each other at this incredible
RATE

life

        clangs on
        TILT

the machine hits
with its incandescent tits

there is the desert
and cactus country
    Love
white as a bone
    with all the delicate hues
      and overtones

BELMONT '78

I

New York
New York again
driving in gritty yellow air
through the clear time passing
Danny and I
who had known each other half our lives
the furtive princely sons of Jewish mothers
still running for our pleasure

Driving through the Barrio
115th St. and Spanish Harlem
on our way to the Belmont Stakes

As if we drove down the bones of old romances
"I used to do social work in this neighborhood, Rich . . .
Used to make love to my clients . . ."
Danny hanging sidewise, snake eyes, furioso
his cigarette clenched between his teeth
romance of blackness
fierce rolling women
soul, electric salsa, broken glass
straight-on surging of that poor angry blood
so seductive to us
        interior middle-class darters
only we weren't kids anymore
but men scrabbling in deep water
and outside the romance was gone
of lives caged to a few square blocks

flattened like scrap or baling wire
in the infernal machines
empty store fronts
stale wine breath
strutting and hard laughter
at the core of a dying star

Danny and I
talking women, money, races
in our closed moving cell
like two heads of the same fear
he hanging tight as a wart
in the city of his birth
I escaped a continent away
veined by phone calls and jet planes
to the anxious stone beebop of the city

And here
crossing the bridge
Randall's Island floating in the East River
Manhattan State Hospital passing on our right
    squat fearsome buildings
rising tan and blunt as hog's teeth

That had been another of our romances
we Jewish schoolboys working as psychiatric attendants
in the brilliant twisted inner jungle
the zoo
garbage hospital
for the poor people of Manhattan island

sadness and terror of who was still there
which of our patients
as if the time had stopped
fifteen years
of jellied animal eyes, devil eyes, dead eyes
imploding
flesh falling to the still helpless center

and behind it the whale itself
stretching to the north and south
theaters, embassies, publishing houses
the tiny jagged buildings like erector sets
unnaturally clear in the sulfurous air
countless tiny people juxtaposed
like planets stacked in cubes
    Leviathan
the humped island of Mind

fading to our backs
as we chattered over the racing form
fading
as we chattered on the past
and I remembered dreams I had as a child
of the humming beast
seen from the inside
all the heads connected
to the subway dragon spine
power junctions rumbling
    down beneath the island
the lemur furnaces
    the secret dynamos

II

Belmont Park spread
      flying for miles
in a peaceful ellipse
wide green circus
of fields and ponds
      candy-striped tents
groves of trees and jets roaring over
thousands of well-heeled people
twittering
rustling their racing forms
betting on the horses

As if the day shifted on translucent gears
of beauty and quick money
and the animals
how they floated onto the track behind the bugle
nervous flaring thoroughbreds
stepping up and back before the stands
anchored to their firm squatty little exercise ponies
floated out in colors round the curve
jittering one by one into the starting gate
and "They're off!"
the hard clear straining
tiny monkey men in silks
      like a Grecian frieze
      an Assyrian lion hunt on TV

Danny and I
still getting by
love boys once again
here at the hot center
glowing at each other
as if our lives leapt
upon these pearls of pleasure
    strung through emptiness

losing and collecting under the sky
in radioactive green Flushing, NY
JFK airport whistling over
beer and food
convivial New York tippling from coast to coast

All building toward the Stakes
effervescence
expectation
of Belmont '78
the third and longest test
for Alydar and Affirmed
Stevie Cauthen the wonder boy
in his shot to sweep

And then
    unbelievably
just before the race
"The Concorde! The Concorde!"
screeching

scrowling up into the sky
a fierce white bird
as big as the moon
so big and piercing
I felt I could hold it
the rippling of its radar muscles
giant alphabets clicking together
squeeze some shape from History
streaming by
in every direction
    like light

III

When they burst from the gate
there came a roar
it was like the rolling of a wave
and they were running free
Affirmed in front
Alydar a few lengths behind
running easily through the first turn

   The day grew suddenly deep
the horses galloping in that wide green field
sound surging
as thousands of people urged them
praying money
    veins and pop eyes
Danny was screaming beside me

and I felt myself lifted out
into a huge crackling bell of energy

    Alydar starting his move along the back stretch
gaining on Affirmed
       gaining
he pulled even coming into the clubhouse turn
and our minds went white

Alive inside the whale
the cruel beast of History
this race created by New York
as surely as Rome made the circuses
winners and the losers
the rich floating
upon crushed heads of the poor
to build these instruments of glory

Alydar and Affirmed running together
neck in neck
sculpted heads locked
in a pure Alexandrine straining
galloping the last half mile
in a pitiless stone stretch
like the pumping of some giant heart

And Affirmed won
again
by a nose

Straight up
Danny and I
hugging each other
punching each other
    electrified
   out of our lives

And when he rode back into the winner's circle
this frail piqued eighteen year old in pink silks
       with his arms full of flowers
he was magnified on TV
and we screamed with the crowd
in that beating hollow
fused together shrieking in release
   for Stevie Cauthen
winner of the Triple Crown

FROM

THE FIELDS

1989

THE CENTER

Drinking coffee on the boulevard
with Carroll the astrologer
and Sal
   returned from long ago
talking Seattle Hawaii
settlements of people we knew
the shine of their eyes
over time and space

   I remembered
a pollenburst of chickadees
in the air rising to the Berkeley hills
catapult into space
the trees breathing
across the crest
like a tremendous pelt

not to need
shelter and center
These eaves are the heavens
This floor our plowed fields
This hearth our wedded love
to be beyond
   flesh
   and nostalgia
in the pure sunlight

THE WORD

He had a
shy chewed up face
drinker ruddy
and losing hair
Told me
after my reading
about teaching at Soledad
how he'd read "Howl"
to those cats
thieves rapists murderers
how quiet they were
pin drop
appreciative grateful
"lambs to the word"
I'd been wandering on the page
a sky
blindness
all messages stopped
Four generations of photographs
on his wall
great-great to his parents
marriages
Southern faces
"Lambs to the word"
he said
and brought me back

Each's Own

a crumbling breastwork   and
lo came lumbering
words in weariness
as in that other poem   you
know   stumbling on crutches past
hospital beds   toward love's
disappearing door

POSTMODERN

swimming here
in the trough of what
's got to be a wave

WILD CATS AND WEEDS

re: poetry as music
it's not abstract
there's a catness to the sound

THE LARGER TIME

Only senses
Not this and this
my half-face cat
calico and black
bare winter persimmon
filled with sparrows
Not the rose bush
sawn at the root
invisible roses
unknuckling   glistening
Not one of these
but many
multiplied
voices   lights
whistling and streaming

I, TOO, DISLIKE IT . . .

the sea crests
around a bend
beyond poetry's
validation and
seen by other heads
other heads
speak to me and we
    suck
   tongues
weave the tongues
and taste the
pearly entropy

GENESIS OF AN ATHEIST

He was a kind
of gray Santa Claus
diffident and blurry
I dreamed him one night
for the first
and last time
As if through a screen door
he spoke to me
but I don't
remember what he said
"You piss me off"?
or was it a secret
like
the true name for 'bird'
like
an emblem of things?
Anyway
some transfer
some spark
And when I woke
God wasn't inside
or outside
He wasn't
anywhere at all

PEARLDIVER'S PALIMPSEST

I was working swingshift
not sleeping enough
awake in a dream
Writing in coffeehouses
my mind would drift
I found myself hearing
the voices at once
the one big voice
barbarbarbarbarbar
progenitive
deep lurking
sea sound
Washing the pots
I'd work through shapes
food stains creeping
eyes hands claws
down to clean metal
the scratches and tarnish
as if that were truth
I got closer and closer

THE HOPEFUL HORSE

Yes
I'm a hypochondriac
but hypochondriacs
have real diseases
Arrested in monkish emptiness
I'm charged with light
and sentenced to bright hell
As a young man I wrung
passion from my situation
now
now I ride it
flogging the hopeful horse

FIRST THINGS

A tooth tingling weewee
or some four year old ur-orgasm
as if I died and
came back again
pressed against the swampy globe
But the globe was Aunt Sadie's girdle
enormous   with a window in it
and she   a raucous Bronx woman
one generation out of Vilna
who wore her stockings
rolled on dumpling white legs
was riding
a red rhinoceros

    long
radius from childhood
I remember this
forty six years old
sliding sideways
in the flesh

POETRY AND REAL ESTATE
AT CODY'S CAFE

for Jerry Ratch

"Selling real estate
is like hunting.
It's OK.
After so long, I
know what I'm doing."
His gaze is even
but as if something is constricting
his insides
"Money. When you do business
with people, then you know them."
Across from us
the burned out hotel
glows   Washed
cloudy sunlight after rain
deepens the greens and reds
organ red of brick
a heavy stubborn color
empty gutted windows
"And then I pry time
for the poetry.
This new book
is good. Really good.
But I can't tell you how hard
the writing was."
Long look   Almost
imploring
"Indescribably hard.

As if I aged five years
to shape it get
something clear
from the murk.
I felt all my grey hairs
sprouting."
He looks at me
in the rainy light
A hungry hollow
As if the poetry
is hunting him

THE FIELDS

As I read
the dream bloomed
and I entered it
He was speaking
"matters of grace"
anastomosing anti-worlds
He evoked
the common dream
so that we were
facets of the zeitgeist
sleepwalkers
puppets but
we could follow our strings
our fracture lines
back into the glow

Gratefully I told him my own
dream visions
climbing through rotten museums
The mortuary dream in which
the lovers mix delicately
as liquids in the grave
Peter's explanations
the dry cerements
lightning hit the evidential pot
The Black girl and Mendelssohn
his music a rustling of angels
Was her angry cry
the world regained?
the angels lost?

the story with its veins popped out
a bum rummaging through
subway trash
"I got to find me some M&M's . . .
something that will keep . . . "
a free man in the nickel package

I spoke these things
to his picture on the back book flap
but
his reaction wasn't personal
He nodded
as if remembering
and just absorbed what I'd said
to further talk
and further writing
How lonely it was then
annihilating
We couldn't mingle
our dreams
We were like
parallel lines
horses grazing past each other
in the fields of intertextuality

MASSING

They were a mother and daughter act
at the poetry readings
both dark
hair and skin
pressed to the limits
of respectability
the little girl aggressive
gypsyish
wanting and posing
coquette   coquette
Now here she is
the mother
parading the avenue alone
in an army jacket
and she's flipped
slipped through
And how do I know this?
The army jacket?
Her furtive vague-eyed walk?
Her face is subtly different
puffy   thickened
like a glove
It seems yellower   Can
that be?   reddish
in its creases
And behind her glovelike
masklike face
it's as though she's lolling
open   sucking on herself
Something obscene   huge and sly

Artaud mountains there   the Momo
his body a black turd
sizzled by electricity
sizzled black in hospital bowels
slick terrifying shit
massing at the hole

TURNOVER

She got on at 21st and Broadway
the sweltering heart
fantasmagoric hooker
in a platinum blond wig
shaggy white fake fur coat
80° in downtown Oakland
and this slim Black lady
seemed cool
lacquered and tinkling and almost kabuki
zombied out and demon dead
Seven blocks to 14th and Broadway
    I forgot her
droning   crowded dream
of breath and sweat
But getting out
I saw a teen-age black kid
shove her through the door
yell something
did she hassle him?
hit on him?
Then as I stepped out the door myself
she shook off her polar bear coat
like lightning
stark naked
at the bus stop
in a crowded ring
pointing and shrieking
fork-eyed   fanged
she hurled her
honey brown cleft body

at the kid
like shrapnel
scraggly small curves and her bush
ripped off her wig
and she was shaven bald
Three cop cars rayed in
on the bus out of nowhere
as I left
Two hours turning
in the downtown gear teeth
I catch the bus to Berkeley
drone past
21st and Broadway
There she is
hanging in the traffic
beyond belief
paid for by whom?
Two hours
bared
busted and booked
and she's on the set again
malicious small pagoda
 in her jewelry   coat   wig

OUTSIDE ELI'S

They've broken into my car
I'm standing around the corner
from Eli's Mile High Club
Night of the blues   spangled glass
Claudia's left for Hawaii
(with a good man at last)
who I first saw on Telegraph Avenue
in 1966
looking like Sheena of the Jungle
who I last made love to on my 37th
birthday   when I was exactly
half my father's age
Like the blues
like Eli's
Claudia unites the black and the white
in sweetness
and pain
in her son Orlando's golden afro
Long flowering stem
of my seedtime
The sixties are gone
Somewhere
far away
the lion lies down with the lamb
They're fucking
Everything gleams
There's a spangled hole
where my right rear window
used to be

"DEALING THE FACES"

1989, UNPUBLISHED

DEALING THE FACES

The cards were an entertainment   a joke
  private wink in the fires of New York
"The Hasidic kids trade them like baseball cards, Rich.
The rebbes!   The superstars!"
Sleek swarthy glow of Steve's face
black hair graying at the temples   flesh
sinking subtly on the bones
Like my own   When I look at him
I see the wreck of the young athlete Steve
my alter ego
who could leap   who could
crack that softball   his horse legs
pounding the beach
A quarter century
cigarettes   spare tire   faint gray beneath the eyes
He handed me the thick small deck
"They believe in them, Rich!
Hasidic masters   *Tzaddiks.*"
"*Tzaddikim,*" Randy corrected him
"They're so funny!" Her brown eyes
beamed   full lips grinning
tongue tip pressed in glee
between her gapped front teeth
Now when Steve and I meet
on my annual trips to see my parents
it's here   in the bosom of his family
his wife Randy   his nine year old daughter Aliza
"The whole line of Hasidic holy men!
All the way back to Rambam—Maimonides!"
Trace of a smirk   almost a leer

Steve's scorn for this religious *meshugas*
these black bowler-hatted Jews
long coats and side curls
who lull themselves on holy men
in the belly of chaos
poverty and street babble
crime   pollution   drugs
At the same time it hooked him
I felt his dark eyes
sparking at me
teased   provoked
by this freakish human intensity
Aliza sat straight
contained   almost inward
spritely small replica of her father
her hair gathered sideways in a glossy
flowery tail
I took the cards and began to deal

As if the soul rose to its dream
out of exile   pogrom   earthly scrabble
not to inwardness exactly
because it was not in space   or time
Like some vast fireball
but perfect
and not burning
Like our own idea
of intense concentration
before the Big Bang
But not   of course

like anything else at all
Ein Sof *Infinite Godhead*

Then   Rabbi Luria tells us
came Zimzum
Because there was potential
not actual
conflict between
good?   and evil?
God contracted
vacated a part of Allself
inhaled   inwardly disappearing
God accepted an exile
so that space and time
could be born

Dealing the faces the cards crept in my mind
quaint portraits   photographs
some retouched in a sepia
unclear zone between
red writing beneath each face
a squiggly Hebrew script
Unlike Steve
furtively   wishfully
I believe in *tzaddikim*
in the secret laws
of human radiance
And so the cards began to nest
to glint and fill with the light of New York

these annual trips
like strobes in a fleshly river

I had met Steve that afternoon
at our regular rendezvous
Printing Trades High School
where he teaches in downtown Manhattan
Every afternoon at 2:30
the school bursts like dropped fruit
like a bomb   The kids explode
out of there   pent up young Blacks and Latinos
streaming
jabbering in twos and threes
punching and hooting and laughing
I saw Steve over the heads waving to me
and we made our way to his brown Toyota
parked on 49th Street out front
got in and began warming it up
cold bright December day   waiting for Lydia
"This might be her last term," he rolled his eyes at me
"Her leg didn't set right. She needs another operation."
I knew Lydia   had met her several years running
as a rider in Steve's Toyota
a member of this harried camaraderie
of warders really   more than teachers
in a vocational school Steve calls a "prison"
bureaucratic zero
whose goals   he says   are survival till pension
keeping the kids in some kind of order
marking senseless violent time

After a few minutes Lydia emerged
blue coat and flowered hat
a tiny monkeylike woman in her mid-sixties
rouged   powdered   inching on her crutches
down the service way behind the school
Steve scurried to help her in
She had gotten a Ph.D. in English from Duke
had taught at Ohio State   and somehow
ended here at Printing Trades
refusing to retire   refusing her pension
although she could have packed it in years ago
I don't remember what we said
pulling out onto 10th Avenue
dodging the taxis uptown
It was always dead air with Lydia
Steve and I
beaming a silent ironic commentary
Lydia a joke   a windup toy
refined good sport repartee
my "vacation" and my "plans"
What stands   looking back
are the buildings where we cross Broadway
around Needle Park
majestic   fortresslike
"How beautiful they are," I said
"Nobody talks about the beauty of New York."
Steve snorted and I remember Lydia's metallic voice
talking about sandblasting
how they'd just get dirtier and dirtier
that there was no pride in the city anymore

"Each one grabs his own, and Devil take the hindmost!"
Suddenly I saw the buildings blackening
as in a furnace
I saw the light bend
on the blackening body of New York
realized
with a feeling of abandonment
floating grief
that my truest sense of time
of my forty seven atom years on this earth
is to see the century move
on this great city where I was born
to see it as if from the air
flying in and out
small as the body of some fabulous beast
And looking back   I see Lydia
not as dwarfish and banal
but as a soul
blank flashing mirror
She was going to spend Christmas in the hospital
an operation to reset her femur
because the pin had slipped
through carelessness   malpractice
And how would she cope
not so much with pain   terror
as with hopelessness?
As far as Steve knows she's alone
without friends or family
living in this brownstone on 77th Street
with two dogs

"I certainly hope you enjoy your stay," she said
rouged wizened monkey face filling the car window
navy coat   flowered hat
dragging slowly through the frame

The second time
God emanated divine light to the world
whose life arose from negation
evil had already fallen
and so the vessels held
giving form
to the lights that flowed within
The lights filled the vessels arrayed
and created the mystical pleroma
the ten sefirot
Tenth and last is Shekinah
God's presence   the feminine element
divine power closest to man
The sixth is the masculine element
Tiferat   *central among the* Sefirot ha-binyan
the powers of construction
And the ninth sefirah
is Tzaddik   *the intermediary*
that flies
between material and divine

Dealing the faces
as if to drink their radiance
as if to steal the wisdom of the *tzaddikim*
I ogled the cards pigfishedly

came on Rambam
it had to be him
line drawing   bearded and turbaned
although the script was foreign
the drawing flat   no spark in the eyes
Moses ben Maimon   *Guide for the Perplexed*
the Rabbi of Cairo
Here was a photograph   somehow elongated
that seemed graven in sadness
the face like rock   hollow-eyed   raging
here a man that looked like Sam Levenson
his milky smiling light
one that looked like a bird with raised crests
vibrant   poised to strike   a hypnotist
The cards have changed in my memory
with all that I've learned about them
I go back and try to match the faces
the Hebrew cursive script
with the famous names
Rabbi Schneur Zalman of Lyady
founder of Habad Lubevitch Hasidism
Rabbi Menahem Mendel of Vitebsk
who migrated to *Eretz Israel*
Rabbi Nahman of Bratslav
the persecuted mystic
A guilty apostate
thirsty for the light
I riffled through these sacred baseball cards
the storied masters   spiritually endowed
and the cards became

a snake of names   skin-splitter
they began to throb in the motion
continuous perfect master
an engine of transcendence
dark and slick

Steve and I had met at eighteen
busboys in the 'Borscht Belt'   at Kutscher's Country Club
and gone through our ritual scarifications
Kutscher's   Sodom in the Catskills
which we left after two weeks
to go back to the city and sell *Collier's Encyclopedia*
where we earned the name "The Golddust Twins"
because we drove out to sell in separate crews
but we always blanked together
sold   even doubled   on the same nights
We had worked together
as psychiatric attendants in Manhattan State hospital
and lost our virginity in the same summer
six thousand miles apart
after having lied about our conquests for several years
the only thing we ever lied about
scaring each other shitless
I remember how we bragged and confessed
late summer in Central Park
laughing   almost crying in relief
rolling in warm grass
beneath the great hazy buildings of central Park West
laid   anointed in the juices   men at last
That afternoon   disembarrassed of Lydia

we flipped back to our mode as the "Twins"
the two running buddies
of paired balanced virtues
an illusion   of course
in what's lost and changing
because I'm still free   as I say
but pounded and shorn
and Steve is a family man
slump-shouldered and thickening
on his round of mercies
"Sorry, Rich—I've got to drive up to Aunt Esther's
before we go home—She has an herbal remedy
she wants me to take out with us to Southampton—
for my father's liver." He gave me a double look
mix of compassion and contempt
like the look he sparked me
when he handed me the cards
"He takes the train in every week for radiation
chemotherapy—maybe it's working—
the tumor's actually smaller.
But she wants to treat him with chicken soup.
I mean, she's a cultivated woman.
She used to be a concert pianist."
Eighty year old Aunt Esther
sending her little brother Matty
a balm against death
His father appeared to me
decades younger   mellowness
scholarly ironies
Steve's younger sister Jane

now more than ten years dead
dancing her mean stiff-legged boppy dance
Romance of the grand concourse
that bustling out-the-window Bronx
As if our lives   Steve's and mine
had spread in some X
of separate incomplete paths
As if the crux had come
when he blew out of his first year of Law school
come back from Indiana with a golden *shiksah*
He sent the wedding invitation to Cambridge, Mass.
I remember kneeling in the shower
folded to a fleshly lima bean
Sunlight   the water pouring on my back
I wept
half in loneliness   half in exultation
The marriage was a lingering disaster
Steve settled with Sue   his bride
in a rent-controlled apartment
his parents got for him on Riverside Drive
the same apartment he lives in now
Six good months
and then six and a half festering years
in which quiet blond leggy Sue
got fatter and fatter
turned catatonic
passive curse
millstone   goiter   round his neck
Steve was paralyzed too
raging   guilty   scared

and the marriage only ended with her hospitalization
"And Aunt Esther wants me to tell my mother
that she won't 'require,'" Steve grinned at me sidewise
imitating his aunt's affectations
"that she won't "require' any chicken.
My mother's so fat she can hardly walk now.
Still, she drives out to this farmer's market
and buys chicken for the world."
Steve's mother
grieving lioness
The two of them have begun a new life
far from the Bronx on the tip of Long Island
in a house that he designed
in which she cooks and quilts
for sewing circles of Christian friends
Matty and May on the shores of the Atlantic
he with the tumor in his liver
she with her sorrow
the dark open secret gnawing on her heart
"I think Esther is really getting dingy.
She hardly leaves her apartment.
To her it's nothing that I drive
all the way up to her place after school
just to pick up a goddamned packet of herbs!"
I could see how tired he was
pinched and gray
how in need of his Christmas vacation
Printing Trades is the anvil he's crumped to
allowed himself to be hammered on
for his family's sake

"You need a rest, Stevie.
And you need some exercise, man,
a program to get yourself
back into shape." How I hated
to see Steve digested
his body sagging   his teeth
rotting in his head
That body I'd been so proud of
whose feats I'd gloried in
as if they were my own
But he answered as I knew he would
that he's too exhausted after school
to even think of exercise
And then he segued to Aliza
monomania   his apple and his garden
"We've bought bikes now.
That's the only exercise I get.
I take her on paths down by the river.
She's so *strong*. She just goes and goes.
It thrills me, Rich, to see that *will* in her."
His helpless dazzled love for his daughter
"I know I'm boring you—but I've got to tell you.
We've enrolled her in gymnastics class—
a pre-Olympic program—
And she's absolutely fearless, Rich!
She can chin herself! She can do a front flip!"
Making his body over to her
Aliza becoming the athlete he once was
Steve's family seized him ten years ago
almost in a fit   an access

"I want to find a nice, Jewish girl, Rich.
I want to get married and have children."
He'd dumbfounded me when he said that
It was just after his sister Jane died
naturally   I thought then   of her diabetes
Steve sitting in the fragments
of another affair   empty   disgusted
offing Mavis   another live-in Black girlfriend
He'd been whirling with dark alien women
Jamaicans   Puerto Ricans   Persians
ever since his first marriage
Passionate women   no future   no threat
night students of his at Manhattan College
women he picked up on the street
who loved his tall dancerly looks
his dark eyes   his powerful legs
"Don't do it," I told him
"Live by yourself, just for a while.
Find out what it's like.
Families don't solve problems.
They just snowball them bigger and bigger."
I the great naysayer
bachelor   therapist   aggressive mouth
But it seems that Steve was right
Two months later he called me in California
He'd met Randy   She was pregnant
And it's been good   It's worked out
Randy is fierce   a warrior
devoted to Steve and her daughter
tough and even with the apartment

money   Steve's parents
That afternoon
buzzing between school and his home
in the Toyota that in fact had been Jane's
her unspoken legacy ·
Steve intoned it again   counted his blessings
"Randy and I are ok together.
The sex is still good."
I could see the old floating threats
spoiled rages   bullying
that began with his mother and Jane
physical violence with Sue
with his girlfriends   lusts   philandering
But he's come through so far
He's made no mess
"We have a simple life.
But I'm content, Rich.
I've never been so content."
Dark nervous eyes
eyes of a deer
peering at me   pressing
as if I disbelieved him
as if   half   he disbelieves himself

The bass tone is exile
the sound in the shadow
because the vessels broke
because the light was lost
From that potential conflict
between good and evil

not stirrings   not itchings
but prefiguration
that caused the first withdrawal
the world stands like a scar
our world removed from Allself
God emanated light
to nourish space and time
but evil lay passive   leaden
and cracks snaked through the vessels
Shevirat ha-kelim
The vessels broke
Imagine the unimaginable
white hot metal in a foundry
white rivers pouring
over dark nonforms
The light was lost
Nizonot   *the trapped sparks*
convulsing here below
were fed upon by evil
because everything is sustained by divine light
even the most vile
even the most lowly

And so   Rabbi Luria tells us
we have entered
now and in the age to come
upon Tikkun
imaged as the union
of Tiferat *and* Shekinah
the masculine and feminine

Tikkun
the mending of what was broken
gathering the light

I was like a thief
with the cards
a hunted animal
Because I believe in the *tzaddikim*
not bearded Jehovah
Adam and Eve expelled from the Garden
the tablets
the two temples
but holiness   primal radiance
Yet   at the same time
I hoarded the power to myself
because I merely shuffled images
sucked at the faces
photographs   even drawings
sucked at the knowledge
the light in their eyes
Giving them motion   a semblance
of life
revving the cogs and wheels
of arcane transcendence
I did what I've always done
Atheist   naysayer
I've held myself aloof
from the earth
marriage   children
daily work

I've sought to swell with power
like an alchemist   a magician
I thirst for the *tzaddik*
and I fear him
terrible master
who will lance my pretences
and open the proud abscess of my life

In fact   though
the cards superbly filled
their entertainment function
They kept us talking right through dinner
"We got them from our friend—
or should I say our acquaintance—
Big mouth Joel. His son, Jeffrey,
got them from a Hasidic kid."
"You really can't believe a thing he says."
Randy beamed, "He's such a liar!"
"It's true, Rich. Joel's an attorney—
big money—and he simply can't tell the truth.
Even if it's a shopping list, he's got to embellish it.
He had a nervous breakdown a little while ago,"
Steve stopped as we thought back
to our dayrooms of patients at Manhattan State
"But don't worry—he's ok—
He's gone back to his practice."
and we chortled over liars as lawyers
"His son Jeffrey's even worse.
For all I know he punched some Hasid
in the mouth and took the cards.

He's twelve years old, and he's a fence.
Hot merchandise.
And he keeps coming on to Aliza.
Tell Rich what he said to you . . ."
Aliza flicked her ponytail pertly
her eyes darkening with the attention
"He says he wants to 'pump my boodie.'"
Her manner was contained   disapproving
but with a twinkle of wickedness
joining in the fun
"He's always try'n'a give me things."
She wrinkled her nose in vexation
Sleek and gypsy-toned
like her father
her slim straight little form
leapt at the center of our circle
A feeling of depth to Aliza
her beauty and pride
bridled by an innate consideration   watchfulness
willingness to please
Steve chuckled uncomfortably
"Yeah—it's a little scary.
I've talked with Joel,
and he knows I don't want Jeffrey
over here anymore.
We kept the cards to show you, though."
Conversation swung
to the Jewish renaissance in cubist New York
how it parallels the Black "Roots" movements
African   Muslim

the Nuyorican   and who knows what other
racial   tribal   spiritual sects
Against that killing grid
intense welter   pullulation
"These rabbis are really superstars!
It's amazing what fame and following they have.
Even my mother almost went to one."
That really amazed me
"She has this friend in Southampton,
Zippy Altman, a Yemenite Jew,
who told her about them. It's because of Jane,
the way she died. You know,
it still tortures my mother.
It eats at her."
Jane had committed suicide
Steve only told me later
after pledging me to strictest secrecy
He said it would kill his mother
if she knew he'd told
"To this day she can't comprehend it.
A failure. A desecration.
As if Jane did it to spite her.
She thinks it's her fault,
that she could have done something.
If she'd only known. If this. If that.
It's maybe only Aliza that's kept her sane."
A synchronicity   a soul hum
between Jane and Aliza
Aliza   poised daring little athlete
conceived almost immediately after Jane's death

Jane had been bloated at the end
her movements wobbling
Her doctors were broaching the possibility
that the diabetes might affect her eyes
But it wasn't the diabetes that killed her
In the depths   at thirty-two
she had taken pills
left no note
after the breakup
of a seemingly meaningless affair
"Aliza knits it together.
They take such joy from her."
Steve caught himself   added hastily
"Not that anything can make up for Jane."
Jane's death had been hard on Steve too
He was haunted with the guilt
he'd been a bad brother
bullied her as kids
been cold and distant as adults
He's never actually said so
but Jane's death surely figured
in his seizure   his surge
for marriage and fatherhood
"My mother would have gone to see the *tzaddik*, too,
but my father was irate.
'What? He's gonna bring her back to life, May?!
He's gonna save her soul!?!'
One of their famous scenes.
You know how my mother is,
the way she drives at things.

She can make you crazy.
And then she prostrates herself before my father,
his mind, his education. Like he's a bird of paradise;
she martyrs herself, the beast, wounded , pouring nature.
That makes him peck at her even harder.
'We'll start *doven*ing, and lighting candles,
and keeping kosher?!'
He gets at her, out of his own bitterness,
'Will you just give it up, May?!
Will you let it finally go?!'"
Despite the painfulness we were all grinning
Aliza giggling at the tones
in her father's voice
The Matty and May sit-com
Steve spends his vacations from Printing Trades
with his parents in Southampton
the whole extended family together
some weeks at Christmas
months in the summertime
in the garden   at the beach
I thought of how I've left New York
of my own parents growing old
in their boxy junior-four apartment in Queens
while Steve has rooted here by Riverside Drive
their intense charging little economy
locked back and forth from Manhattan to Southampton
three generations
the Southampton house bequeathed
to Steve and Randy   to Aliza
"I love Zippy, though,"

Randy was bringing hors-d'oeuvres
in from the kitchen   crackers   cheese   caponata
while we sipped burgundy and the lasagna baked
"Tell Richie about Zippy."
"Oh, yes, Zippy is a formidable little character!"
He pursed his mouth
"Zippy for *zipporah*. That means 'bird' in Hebrew.
She comes from Yemen. Dark.
They look like Puerto Ricans.
My parents' only Jewish friend in Southampton.
She's a learned woman, Rich,
a professor of Near Eastern Studies.
She has this very no-nonsense manner."
Steve assumed a serious expression
accompanied by brisk wrenlike gestures
"She marches out onto the beach. Bikini. Shades.
She picks her spot, digs a little hole for herself,
wriggles right in, and that's it for the afternoon—
she reads her *New York Times*."
"I like Zippy because I can talk Hebrew with her."
Randy poked her head out of their small kitchen
"She bent my ear about the *tzaddikim*."
Randy had been a secular Zionist
lived and worked in *kibbutzim*
At twenty-four   when Steve met her
she was a conservatory musician   a cellist
But both those pursuits have been swallowed
without ripple
into the body of their marriage
Seemingly by her own calm choice

she wants only to be Steve's wife now
Aliza's mother
Burgundy in hand   I slipped into the kitchen to quiz her
"Well, I remember what Zippy said.
She's so vivid! First of all,
there's no such thing as a freelance Hasid."
An image of the Messiah scattered in pieces
like seeds   to each time and place
and around each seed a community grew up
a Hasidic court
Instead of one final magnificent *tikkun*
gathering the sparks of the broken world
the *tzaddik* performs daily *tikkunim*
With his flock   he furthers the work of redemption
"Zippy thinks that they're all heros, 'sacred athletes,'
she said   But they draw their strength
from their community, from the people's belief in them."
the *tzaddik* 'sins for the sake of heaven'
Righteous himself   he confronts sin
and uplifts it
He is the intermediary
The people give him material support   his livelihood
and he soars for them to the uppermost worlds
draws down divine emanation
But he can't stay above   united with *Ein Sof*
He must come back down
and rejoin his people
"What a gorgeous idea!" I burbled
"It's like the *boddhisattva*! like Christ!"
Randy made a face "I don't like the Hasidim.

They're so ugly! Those dark colors and the curls.
They seem so—old-fashioned and joyless."
Matter-of-fact   practical
her vision simplified and concentrated on her own
her family   progressive Judaism   Israel
Steve thinks it has to do
with her fatherless only-childness
Her father left her mother when she was a baby
Deprivation   Anger
She blinkered and stopped down
to cope with his absence
We trouped into the dinette
The lasagna was ready
But as we ate and drank wine
Randy kept remembering tidbits of Zippy's disquisition
"The *tzaddik* also bestows earthly riches,
long life, and sustenance, and sons."
She cackled, "Zippy says a *tzaddik*'s true greatness
is measured by the fertility of the wives!"
Randy's friendship touches me
the fierce privilege of her acceptance
warm   simple   incurious
I'm Steve's best friend
a part of her family
We began telling Hasid jokes
screwing in lightbulbs
whores covering their cunts with *yarmulkes*
"Oy vay! Moishe slipped!"
Aliza listened and laughed
and seemed very much entertained

However she sees me   her funny yearly uncle
Wine   the hilarity
I felt a stirring
Steve   open   and flushed   and relaxed
as if we were all moving
a river of time   changing faces
I thought of the *tzaddik*'s solitary ascension
his ladder teetering against the stars
"Zippy's amazing," Randy enthused
"She knows each and every one of them!"
"She does, Rich," Steve looked at me
"She disputes with them
like they were her teachers!"
"While we were talking she picked up the cards,"
Randy imitated the gestures
"and she went through the whole deck,
real fast—bing! bing! bing!—
dealing them out into two separate piles
all the time saying—you know, Steve,
the funny way she she talks—
'Livink! dett! Livink! dett!'"

FROM

TOTEM POLE

1996

FOR POETRY

"Momma   I wanted to take you
into the uncreated
Bee and wasp
Dog and cat
Man and woman"   I wrote
and it was false
My mother lay
in her rose-colored bedroom
in her bra and pantyhose
her body old   and soft
and fat as a baby's
In the silence
the glint of her mirrors
I bred a long-legged fly
doubled it monstrously
let it mime itself on the waters
I bred it for poetry
I said that her breasts
pointed like guns
that my father spun around us
moony smile
empty bed   ashes
hiding in the closet
The thought had been sneaking
hunting me
that my mother
was growing demented
But that
was the silence of our separate natures
a raging infection

the fruit of neglect
My mother was wandering
dehydrated
a lonely old woman   loveless
who painted her face for the doctor
I wrote
that she was a harlot
succubus
black crush at the heart
And why did I say that
for poetry?

NEMO

Sound of the creek rushing
in the full moon light
the wee hour traffic
sighing in and out with the surf
off the flank of California
Hours before
making love
we heard a sound like GROK-GROK
saw a raccoon through the scrim
of the open tent flap
standing on his hind legs
sniffing in
peering in
and then their shadows running past
Now her face in the glowing
seems blissful
open as a map in sleep
And I'm up
my head nattering   puzzling it out
That boy in New York
who dreamed himself a banished king
no one in the moonlight
who never came back

WATER

Because I knew
that's what he wanted most
had raced his death
to revise his books
because I wanted him
to die happy
however strange that idea
a moment at an edge
swallowed in nothingness
"You're a poet" I said
His eyes opened like a doll's
rolled to flat focus
"Napoleon?"

I'm writing this on the computer
he put the bug in my head
to buy
blinking cursor
dream horse

his wife's face
bony wreath around
her tender eyes

his family of red-haired
children   and grandchildren

his own face   shrewd   Jewish
licked with humor

the poetry

I might be writing about those things

But it's that final wraith
that fascinates me
end
the flickering of my own
bad faith

It was like bending over water
speaking down into water
". . . poet . . . poet . . ."
I repeated inanely

Owl

Judy and I
and Don and Alice
only Don is dead
and that's the point   flat black
cutout   his own power animal

We're taking Alice out to Party Sushi
only the three of us to love and shine
the occasion:
editing Don's Owl book

"Don was always good with languages
like those Sid Caesar Carl Reiner routines
nonsense with a good accent
And we had a friend
who actually knew French
but his accent was terrible
Between the two of them
we did alright . . ."

Owl   Don's beat the cancer
visioning spirit
whose presence is absence
clouds eating clouds
feathered glints in the corner
of your eye

Judy and I were still lovers
when Don was dying

It's all
heaping together in my mind

Spider rolls   Berkeley
Dynamite rolls with their tomato red
flavor eyes   like the face cards
of our poker games   kings and queens
one-eyed jacks   magical
fate-woven numbers

Alice is so even   so tender
and strong   Just tonight
just once in all this time
I saw the glint of tears
When I mentioned having a memorial
reading for him at Cody's
And Judy is good at drawing her out
like a daughter with her mother

". . . That was just before we had Noah
and Don was starting the Print Mint
on Telegraph Avenue
We had people working for us—
some of them are still working there—
and we were sharing space with Moe . . ."

We're all munching
dipping our sushi in the sauce
Judy is striking her familiar
gossipy poses   like looking at her

through a pane of glass   odd
Owl presence   although of course
we're not talking about the book

Don's dying bonded the four of us
those last few months
when the cancer was blooming
inside his bones   odd
what a wonderful time we had
drinking wine   munching on Alice's
"funny dinners"   Don and I
reading our poetry back and forth

He was in a rage
to put together his unpublished books
especially the Owl book
his vision healing   he was in a rage
of poetry   unable to write
through the morphine
mourning his little boy self
athlete boy   fast
who could jump car hoods
little could fly boy

"Moe leased a space in a building
on Haight and Ashbury
Moe was quite a live wire in those days
He was younger   political
he had more energy
not so clamped down on business

And they wouldn't give him his use permit
They thought he was a trouble maker
had radical attitudes . . ."

Don's absence   dazzling
He's almost sinister
the way we fear the dead
as if he was angry I
was living when he was dying
poetry   or poker
Coyote tongue laughing

Judy puts her hand lightly
on my back while she talks
Alice is laughing
her bony Minnesota face
evangelical parchment

Judy knew Don mostly
from our three weekly poker games
bluffing each other
or sandbagging
our gossip and jokes
Don shrewd behind his cards

And Alice only played with us once
She and Don went head to head
on the biggest hand of the night
raising back and forth
eyeballing each other

and he folded
because she really believed
her full house with two aces
beat his full house with three kings

"That was the beginning
of the Summer of Love
all those store fronts opening up
everything was happening—
fifty arrests a day—
and they *still* wouldn't give Moe
his permit . . ."

Judy has that hooded look
she gets when people talk about
the 60s   the decade she was born
and I'm thinking about the times
level on level   So bright and close
irrecoverable

Don told us he was terminal
at one of the poker games
that it had gone from the prostate
to his bones   and people were
stopped   fumbling for platitudes
slipping into a morbid funk
"Life! . . . Death!"   Don said
with his mild solid smile
"Let's play ca–a–ards . . ."

Coyote and Fox
Magpie and Owl
played poker above us

the little boy that owl fluttered out of

but Owl wasn't Don
Owl wasn't Don's Other
He called up the poetry
hopeful emptiness

"We were living in the front
keeping the space for Moe
and people were squatting
in the back   God   the craziness
Everything blew through there
All those people
the music   the drugs
I could show you a picture
of that place in *Life* magazine . . ."

Hard curve of its passage
people like wind or leaves
Listening to recordings of Janis
brassy   yearning
knowing that she died and how

On the drive back
Alice turns nervously to me
"At the memorial reading . . .

I just want our friends there.
The people who really knew him . . ."
Streetlights running her pale face
I assure her   tell her the names
thinking of that poets' dream room
lined in books and author's pictures
all the readings   Don's
among them

Noah and Kahti back at the house
staying with her
Kahti's pregnant
We have coffee and Kahti's Finnish pastries
The living room is transformed
no hint of that last time we saw it
Don on the raised hospital bed
picking at himself feebly
laboring for breath

And we're a little nervous
huddled on the porch   a little
hollow   saying goodnight
because we don't know
when we'll see each other again
I say a few words
about the Owl book   how good it is
about a possible publisher

We beam at each other
but we're pointing north
three compass needles

MUSIC

Sunny Saturday
and I'm trapped
as ever and ever
in the great bones
   of my skull
Minds seething all around me
The Latino woman across the street
that I spy on
through my scrim curtain
and lust after
mestizo   rangy   androgynous
what's this Saturday morning
like for her?
trundling down her front steps
with her brown little girl
My friend Jerry
whom I haven't seen in months
he lives only blocks away
his domed white head
of shipyards   and wiring diagrams
the news behind the news
I've always been haunted
by All-the-Minds
Does it have entity?
like a tree   say
giant monkey puzzle
shimmering in the sun
Charles Brown
is singing the blues on my radio
His voice

so intricate with what he knows
And the music
that knows more

POETIZING AT THE MED

"What's that—a big list?"

I'd just got it down   a poem
to sandbag night's furious flow

and he's razzing my
superannuated WCWilliams machine
flush left
jumpy line   line   line

not fast and disjunct
'the new sentence'
the art train
slick and gone
past the faces

just the old
Imagist poem
get down
what you see

Stab the present as
it flows off your fork

GEORGE HACKETT SIMPSON AND THE THREE SAD CIGARETTES

"I'm too old—
I'm too old for this shit!"
as if he could step off the street
his face like gutted flame
into a school for accountancy
limps close on a bad knee
to hit me up for change
and stays to embroider his life
Nam   an improbable
Ph.D. in Physics
rambles in Japanese honor families
"wouldn't back down to no one"
and blurs to a glow
the coming of The Hero
He hits on a street dude for three cigarettes
then refuses one to a pockmarked black man
who begs him to buy it
with some pennies in a cup
pops back at me
ferret intense
"Fuckin cops" he says
"fuckin cops"
red dime on his cheek
the size of a bullet hole
"keep telling us to split—
they don't even know what
reality is"
With fawning eyes
he arrogates reality to us

him and me
dreaming atolls
We beat for a while
together in the street lights
the silent night air

FROM THE INSIDE OUT

The performer enters her cage
and starts to climb
She's reading old poems
depending on starpower
   casual   silky
but she doesn't know
if it'll work this time
And the audience
hovers on her in the lights
Pale in her vampire makeup
lank black hair
she'd be skinny
ratlike
if it weren't for
her humor   and nerve
revving too high
her confiding inside laugh
with its drug spine shiver
which all create a
leggy hypermodern look
The audience breathes closer
And she's climbing now
out of that Chicago suburb
that she misfit in every way
lesbian   homely
soulful   smart
working the power of strange
stripper   and witch
druggie   and rebel
And the audience is on her

with her
It breathes back and forth
a great love egg
She's something
hatching in the lights
like a beautiful insect
up
through shit and blood
gism and sex juice
eating her way from the inside out

THE GOLDEN GATE

Drizzling clown
guttering diva
but luminous
love creature
I'm trying to understand
these heartbroken poems for Artie Mitchell
slave poems   how else to say
love poems
Maybe he was Christ
Probably he was just the bald
sandy punk in the paper
who projected no light
(shadow   absence in your poems)
shot to death by his
punk brother   Mitchell brothers
cufflinks of the SF porn industry
I'm trying to remember the story
you told of distance and speed
being chauffeured across the Golden Gate
cocaine and slavey sex
Distance
between actual fucking
and screensized cocks and cunts
performer and audience
self and horizon
All I can understand is distance
yearning across a gap
loving the loss
by losing the other
sucking the loss
the bullet hole

PERSONIFIED

Here comes Xavier Cugat
striding weirdly out of my childhood
Once he was bumble bee
the rhumba man

On the rug
before the wooden console radio
my blood thrilled to his music
rhumba jungle rhumba jungle
prowling   baring my teeth
becoming a panther

Now Cugat's huge and changed
his glossy dark eyes
beneath humped camel brows   eyelashes
humped camel nose
have grown vague and smudged
His ripe piggy wife
paid for in panther money
in bandleader's millions
dancing   shaking her
concentric jellies
is a sad old woman now
raining down fat
and Cugat is dead

Let him go   Let Cugat go
It's raining in the rhumba jungle
and his name is weird
Xavier Cugat
time weirdly personified

ZEALOTS

"What would you do if you
found someone who didn't believe in God?"
we'd ask each other gleefully
Bomb them
Dynamite them
Chop them in little pieces
and pee on the pieces
But one day I asked my mom
"Richard, you have to
respect other people's beliefs,"
she said
So I had her
bossy Sylvia   older   bigger
who was always one-upping me
who always took the starring roles
in each and every one
of our only child's games
dominant female gorilla
to my runty subservient male gorilla
Sheena of the Jungle
while I had to be Sheena's
inept dopy boyfriend Bob
"Sylvia," I asked her expectantly
"what would you do
if you found someone who
didn't believe in God?"
Somehow
        to this day I don't know how
she answered
"Richard, you have to respect

other people's beliefs."
Is it any wonder then
that I punched her in the mouth
at Sanford's instigation
when she was twelve
that when she was eight
and I was six
I stuck my big toe
into the soft fat juncture
        of her thighs
and tickled what I now know
was her cunt
while she rolled her eyes
and screeched helplessly
or   in front of both our parents
that I tried to strangle her
leaped and got a forearm choke hold from behind
as they watched   thunderstruck
Sylvia staggering beet-faced
in the hallway
while I clenched my teeth and squeezed
dangling on tiptoe down her back
like a papoose on its squaw

THE OLD NEIGHBORHOOD

Terror was fat in my life
Electric bison Broadway
The ripe carcass of Washington Heights
was mine to explore
Tubes like intestines
phallic
subway tunnels
elevator shafts
our long hallway
flooded with darkness
that seeped up from bloodbanks
    Egyptian crypts
And there were alleys
playgrounds
the river and rocks
creeping with tough mean kids
Irish Italian brown
kids and black
Here I am pop-
eyed with terror
trapped in an entrance court
by Puerto Rican Danny
who's built thick
head puffed like a tomcat's
who wants to hurt me
"I gonna break yo' face"
And I pump like a gland
I glow like a jewel in the gut
of that vast magical body

Dream Body

A coach of voices
whispering in all
its springs and axles
That's it
though you can
surmise battling forces
Just the expectant carriage
rolling
Its great shadow
birds along beside it

Five Questions for the Postmodern Poet

If poetry is a love feast   are the poets meat puppets?

If my father is dead   if when I was six years old
I leapt out of sleep in the pouring sun
what then?

Begin with your intensely lived experience
Mask it   mask it
Will it play in aporia?

She took off her clothes   Paler places
She was 5'8"   tall and round as a tower
"Baby, baby, baby," she said
"take me down   I'm so blue"
Who am I?
What's that girl to you?

So to Speak

Poets shed light
the way snakes shed skins
new forms
new lives
Bird and Snake
fought for Man's soul
said a New Guinea poet
Bird won
That's why men die
Tangled in wires and
numbers now
poets shed light alone
        I   we
Je est un autre
so to speak
we've got bulbs to burn

TOTEM POLE

When the crack snaked through
when the bill came in on our loving
I starting thinking
beginnings fast forward to ends
all the relationships
squashed ass to head
a totem pole
carved love stick
a spine
on which my flayed skin hung

I turned inside
(my mother aching
like a star
my father
nowhere to be found)
I wanted to stay inside the love body
I wanted never
to come out

thub-dub   thub-dub
in the pale ache of aging
my heart counted
each carved face

MANDALA

I'm only happy
when I'm sad

flesh gets slammed
in the doors of childhood

our mandala

apple
of your hips
straddling me
I'm up inside
your eyes
are closed
sucking my lips like a bee

Hamlet's pun about
"country matters"

cunt tree

DRIFT

Father's Day 1992
and Poppy's gone in time
tumbling
covered in sun writing
The horses shake their manes
He understands poetry
now as he didn't in life
Nothing to
hold to
Poppy is tumbling
in a musical 40s
And I'm a
fatherless poet
at a dashboard
of the century
I mirror my eyes
I see my soul
a speeding electron
an unclarity

STEERING THE TRAIN

There were wheels
in the cars of the old IRT trains
we took to our adventures in Times Square
That comes back
bright sliver from our playworld
It rolls away
from the image of my father
in a hospital bed
in diapers
raising his arms to God
to help him shit
arms so white and wrinkled
they look like empty sleeves
There's no magic in my father's death
There's no no in the unconscious
Pop said that they were steering wheels
that I could steer the train
So I'd swagger to the front car
ahead of him
and he strolled behind
smiling on his sonny
I knew I wasn't steering
The tracks
and how would the train go
when I wasn't riding?
Still I doublethought a spirit steering
that my father gave me
like a pinball game in the underworld
If we hit it right
the train racketed in the black tunnel

speedsparks   no red or yellow
    all green
into Grand Central Station
that was   just as it said
a kind of pelvis

When I bent to kiss my father
goodbye in the hospital
I got the same stubble feel
as when I was a little boy
flying in his lap

stubble   subway   cemetery

It reminded me of steering the trains
Just before we swooshed in
sudden light   crowded platform
other tracks flashed for an instant
split off
ghost axis
at an angle in the dark

1650 Broadway

The Great White Way   photo on her refrigerator
looking north on Broadway from Times Square
40s cabs   shiny rainy look
to the pavement
I felt something begin to flow
cut loose from our unsayable particulars
"A pretty girl is like a melody"
the sound of traffic
windy sound of years
glint of them
faces and faces
alien and young and just around a corner
from familiarity

My father's office was up there
1650 Broadway
nested in those blocks of buildings
singers and dog acts   comedians   boxers
He might have been up there   bullshitting on the phone
sharp sweet face
somewhere in the interference patterns
the waves and bouncing waves of rainy light
that made that photograph
My father in the larger
rise and fall of New York Jewish music   show biz
"To let my Daddy go
to feel the cats   the rhythm flow
the black girls dancing in a row"
Only that was a power vision
like when I was a kid

and saw my bones on Dr. Chomski's fluoroscope
I'd slip my hand behind the screen
and there they were
    carpals   metacarpals
mortal hand
But in the hospital
I saw his bones with my naked eyes
the orbits of his skull

And where does she come in
my baby   my young lover?
Contingency only
touching
like when my mother called us in Berkeley
at 2 AM
her gutted voice
"Your pop is dead"
We had just come home
were getting ready to make love
and she threw her body down on mine
held us touching down our lengths
hard
as if she were holding me together
split screen between flesh and bones
Contingency
like the photo on her refrigerator
a key
an avenue

We never were your typical
Norman Rockwell father and son
"Daddy and Sonny" was his phrase
He was more my playmate
"My two boys" my mother called us
I always knew she loved me more   most
And I never was afraid of him
He only hit me once
when I called my mother a "dirty pig"
He slung me ferociously over his shoulder
carried me up the long hall to my room
I felt him melting with each step
The rage had been mostly for Mommy's benefit
In my room he dumped me on my bed
tapped me with his belt buckle
and fled
The flip side was I never respected him
I was ashamed of him
my timid daddy
who always wanted to
"go home to Mommy"
when things got tough
who told me   turning seventy
of his terror in the subways
     strangers   the closeness
that he'd lose control
and shit his pants
who told me later   well in his eighties
of his stuttering as a boy
of his fear of people that he masked

in the drinking that made him brave
He felt like a "failure" in his life
a "coward" because he never
"made a million dollars"
because he chose instead to be liked
"Honest Al"   roasted by the Lambs Club
stood to drinks in every bar on Broadway
But my father's special genius was his silliness
"Did you get my drift
or do I have to snow again?"
"A pretty gi-i-rl is like an elepha-a-ant"
If you asked him "What?"
he'd say "Turkey trot"
When I called him "Pop"
he'd call me "Shmop"
And he babbled   talked baby talk
not so much for Mom and me
he was his own man in the fullness
of his pleasures
but in our company
with us as audience
Perhaps his masterpiece
—I transliterate—was
"Gock giddy geek gock   gook-gook-gook"
He was a profoundly silly man
The particular brilliance of this phrase
is that   with minor variations
it's a universal lyric
It goes with any tune
Try it with the tune of your choice

And so I babble too
speechify   necromancy
of the saving metaphor
stare decisus
starry deceased
To let my daddy go

I hated him briefly when I was fourteen
pumping in urgent modelless macho
but that exploded   quickly passed
and I loved him tenderly as he became an old
and then a very old man
Pop   Poppiddy I called him
reversing the baby talk
or just Poppy   like a flower

He was listed in a couple of histories of the Catskills
my brilliant historical daddy
He played piano during the Depression
in almost every state of the Union
on cruises to Rio de Janeiro
with Ramona and her Men of Music
He knew Milton Berle   Buddy Hackett
Barnie Ross   Little Augie Pisano
Desi Arnaz   Sid Caesar
Richard Pryor

Love squirming with shame

I list his accomplishments

Were you scared, Pop?
Did you go down the tunnel
see that trendy white light?

When she and I took our first weekend trip
to sit the house of a friend in Marin
deck   hot tub   gorgeous view
my father was two weeks dead
We woke up in the loft bedroom
underneath a skylight
and made love
Intense first wonders of the body
rooting hard there   with her
like a newborn pig that thinks
he's almost home
And then we put on Johnny Otis
our favorite rhythm and blues show
and Johnny was playing Memphis Minnie
There was no particular association
lying close   high flutter of leaves
blue sky
I suppose anything
could have reminded me of my Poppy
Not his kind of music   too funky
But he might have dug it
Johnny was saying he just
found out she died
Mrs. Minnie Overton
a few years ago in a nursing home in California
And then her voice came on

hard party voice of a woman in midlife
singing about her wild youth
"In My Girlish Days"
And suddenly   with a lurch
like leaning over a high space and
dropping something
he was gone
Or more precisely
sunlight on Bronx streets
foods and smells and faces
I'd always known that he and I
were strangers
who could only touch in play
But I'd felt his life there for me
available
just around a corner
There was a moment in the hospital
my father lying there in diapers
like his worst subway nightmare
white   as if whitewashed
but mottled too
the final pink and white old man
that I saw his family resemblance
He was the youngest of five
all girls   all dead   above him
I looked at his brows
and I saw his mother there   Buba Lena
I saw my aunts   his sisters
all spinning through those bony sockets

collapsed in time
like a litter of cats

He's been dead almost a year now
I look at the picture on her refrigerator
and I think of him on Broadway
in the 40s
the club date agent's happy hunting ground
But that Marin moment still sticks
crawling between noheaven
a long sky to fall down in
and earth
slow stone roll

FROM

DOUBLENESS

2000

PHENOMENOLOGY

Morning BART station
The screen blinks on and off
 FREMONT   FREMONT   FREMONT
but the train doesn't come
An eerie expectancy
The face of the tunnel
seems to change as we stare
    green lights
muffled roar of the air conditioning
A stillness poised on the lip of birth

How many centuries
have we philosophers been waiting?
"Our inquiries should be directed . . .
to what we can clearly and perspicuously behold
and with certainty deduce;
for knowledge is not won
in any other way."
We crouch before that blinking portal
 I THINK THEREFORE I AM
methodically doubting
sifting the stony air
but the train
never comes swooshing in
    never   never
tiger face   the Ideal

THE CROWS

Frank decided to commit suicide
He was sick of his rosy drinker's face in the mirror
        fat
        and drooping like a basset hound's
of his phlegmy voice
and his ex-high school gymnast's chest
that had rock slid to his belly
        sick of his bunged-up $100 cars
compression shot   popping along like tea kettles
of playing bachelor games with women
whose minds seemed like mouse traps
or one-way mirrors
empty incomprehensible games
        that he tired of   or lost

He drove out into the winter country around Somerville
out into the birches and oaks
He had taken off his belt when he looked up
and he saw black forms   flitting
thought that they would shit on him
        after he died
that they would dart down and feast on his eyes

He started cursing
alone in the whiteness
shouting blood pumping
a short strong Irish man throwing snowballs at the crows

ONCE AGAIN

Two years in my red pedestal room   excavating for magic
while the time drained evenly away

    the rosebush   scarecrow in the yard
epiphanies at sunset

lovers in this sullen room   tomcats and ghosts

the sound of traffic
descended on silvery escalators

a big throat
grande gueule

ROSENCRANTZ AND GUILDENSTERN

I woke up like an apple falling from a tree
had dreamt of Robert   Rosencrantz and Guildenstern
a different dream play
urban   faggot   socio
     S & M
Robert was the director
As before
in golden summer
when we did our play
I had been the director
     before his wasting
nervous disease
dizziness
   paralysis unto death
      that they couldn't diagnose
and in the dark turbulence of sleep
we had changed places

The Audience

Redemption? because they loved me? or loved me in my words?
   intelligent faces soulful pricked for the poetry

   And that night a woman came in a dream Indian or black
aging alone the phrase "ghosts in her eyes"
   "I'm a perfect case for attention," she said
   So I was listening to her words pained dry fretful driven
writing them down for the poetry   that disappears
   She seemed flattered not realizing
the flat of the language   its tundra
   I was flattered too not realizing her own need
         simply to speak
   "Loaves of bread," she said

   The next morning I saw   loaves were love risen
their faces amazed that we know someone in dreams
   wandering in tundra   redeemed

DREAM OF THE HAND

Gouging into my hand deep inside
    probing for jewels there
An itchy necrotic pleasure
    like digging for stuffing
        in a turkey

My hand I say
    but it floated in front of me
size of a large dog
    in a tunnelworks a mineshaft

    Alarm   dread
thought I'd destroyed my hand
    Light was shining through it

And then it was gone scampering
    in the tunnels
not mine anymore
    monkey's paw Morse code
        tapping   scratching

As the dream bends to daylight
a meaning seems to smile
Out an airplane window
the tunnels start to spell something
    huge and familiar

I've wanted to open that riddled hand

    shining holes
        a scattering of hand words

legerdemain   maintain   manoeuvre   manifest

DOUBLENESS

for Heather McHugh

Two black boys
carrying a ten foot snake
See how they tip and swagger
little boy sorcerers
the cloudy line of bush behind them
Is the snake for show power?
to sell?
to eat?
The photographer though
has caught them (posed them?)
reflected in a mudflat pool
The snake curlicues
across their shoulders
above and below
perfect symmetry
struck and split
And yet the boys
and their reflections are not
the same
The faces frown
impassive   tilted
all shrewd theatre
But their dark
unconscious doubles
flat against a hazy sky
seem bigger   faster
The silhouettes boomboom
They swing across Africa

the big snake pomp
the night fear
Tricksters bearing snake meat
they are a gift
freely moving
Doubleness
Art   and the spirit world
what we say
and what we mean

SUBWAY

I knew I'd never hear
  the end of it
taste the slate blue
    steel blue
      end of it
crawling the third rail
tempting the tunnel's black gullet

Martin and Osa Johnson's Africa

Black man running
in the wide gray veldt
fast
faster than I'd ever seen
stick legs just
twinkling in terror
and the lion
bounded after
lazy it seemed
but cutting the distance
springing gathering
springing
until it pulled him down
kicking in the high grass
It was the first
real death I'd seen
Even in long shot
through Martin and Osa's camera
it was real
death
and funny
He was a nerve clown
sprinting there
futile nameless
tree of scream
Did they set him up?
roll-eyed scar-faced
black gunbearer
Or was it an accident and they

stood by filming
in their pith helmets?
What if that had been
Victor Mature?
I didn't question though
On film it was slick
as a menu
I just peeled my eyes
thrilled
as the lion bounding behind
licking its chops
to taste death's sweet meat

Different

When he was six his
eyes froze in the mirror
He saw that other people's
darted rolled slid
in their heads
But his were
frozen in the mirror
still stare

THE GORILLA WOMAN

It's the changing moment I remember
not the plot: circus setting
trans-
planting the gorilla heart
to save her (soon
to be reclaimed by darkness
and death)
not her lover
the animal trainer
but the horror moment
when she looked into the mirror
and changed to a gorilla
They exploited
transformation
blast furnace of the fairy tale
Even as a woman she was
different   darker then
more febrile   carrion
sweet
wilder   lower   sexier too
But for years
I was haunted by that moment when she changed
frail desirable lovely woman
growing dark   hairy
fearsomely strong
crossing beast boundaries and
    sex boundaries too
Once gorilla
she was wholly female again
But I forgot the sad romance

of her sex
how she tried to save the animal trainer
her lover
from a lion
how they shot her carrying him
unconscious in her arms
grotesque and doomed
a woman trapped within a beast
I remembered only the moment of power
human to animal
how her nose grew flat
and opened
how her face began to smolder
in black hair

HEAVEN

Mrs. Kavanaugh trudges with her bag of groceries
up the piss-smelling stairs
pausing at each landing to catch her breath
Her pulse pounds in her ears
Her ankles are swollen
her feet painfully
loaves in an oven
She fumbles for her key in the dim hallway
and lets herself in the double-locked door
Inside it is cool
the curtains drawn
odors of boiled cabbage and the cats
Gratefully she sinks into the easy chair
the bag between her knees
and stares up at the mantle
the picture of Arthur in his soldier's uniform
next to the picture of Jesus
his lush red heart
The cats come purring
rubbing on her calves
but for the moment she ignores them
This is her time alone with Arthur
before her husband comes grunting from work
his beer and cigar smoke and demands
To be alone
to reabsorb him to her sunken body
Nothing can make up for the death of a child
Not her other children
not the grandchildren
At first his death was jagged

as if they had ripped his blondness out of her
            searing
as if she were birthing him again
But now it is almost a comfort
round   a foreshortened space
like an altar niche inside her
Vaguely   it becomes her own death
the bright pool of heaven

NEAR SANTA FE

Killing time
getting out of her angry house
he strolled down the road
towards the redroof church
It sat in a hollow
the road twisting around her house
and down
As he descended the slope
the building slowly rose
wooden with a blaring metal roof
and what turned out to be a churchyard
full of old people
tending the graves on a Sunday afternoon
a couple of old men in sombreros
working with rakes and spades
and a gaggle of old women
with watering cans and wreathes of flowers
They looked Chicano
or Indian perhaps
seemingly busy and happy
as if they were having a peaceful party
He raised his hand as he drew close
almost in a gesture of commendation
Some of them saw him
nodded back   haha
Strange and lovely
he thought   continuing past
to know each other
so many slow years
to gather in the name of their dead

The wreathes were like a touching
at every point
as if their circles
united the wide earth and sky
The road took another sharp bend
and he stopped in his tracks
A horse was grazing in a field
in front of a broken down barn
They seemed to echo each other
shaggy patched hide
blistering paint
Both the animal and the building
were swaybacked
Nobody around
Silence   except for the wind
the horse's snufflings and munchings
Angry as he was   unslept
         adrenaline pumped
he felt himself opening
crossing a border
into the land of dilapidation
    languid   intimate
She had suggested that he go to see the church
before their fight   the bitternesss
and he thought how funny it was
that even now
sick to death of her
of her scorn   and intolerance
he was secretly pleasing her
improving himself

and she would never know
He strolled a little farther
to where the view spread
a field flanked by rolling low hills
and listened to the wind
When it blew
it turned up the silvery
underblades of the grasses

On his way back
maybe fifteen minutes
he passed the old people in the churchyard
smiled toward them
But they avoided his eye
seemed uneasy
More than it should have
that hurt him
but he realized
he was an intruder
Roads are for going places
not for Anglo tourists
to march up and down on
peering into our lives
did they think?
Or did they just blip him
like a cow or a mosquito?
Still he imagined looking through their eyes
seeing the house above
dominating the ridge
It was built on a slant

the front on higher ground
than the back
which   from this angle
gave it a too tall look
as though it were bunching to jump
Clean and square in the landscape
an ugly jumping Anglo house
He remembered when she had left him
to take a job
to come live in this "psychic" land
and "seek her soul-mate"
How pathetic
plunked above this languid ancient poverty
rectangular
middle class
'new age'
And after buying this plot
designing and building
she even had the nerve
to resent the new houses springing up around her
breaking her view
And yet   of course
he was pathetic too
seeing only her ridiculousness
picking at it like a scab
she who had been for him a glowing darkness
a "stunned dreamy tenderness"
God   the power of falling out of love
that he had survived   survived
the loving of her

For the moment
he felt neither angry nor sad
only elated
and beneath   a sense of blessed numbness
Climbing back toward her house
he drank the landscape with his eyes
to hold it
bring it back with him
on his flight to California next morning
the redroof church
wind   restlessly combing
a ghost horse
in bright spaces

THE PAGE

Words are separating
from things
You can feel them losing reference
bleeding goodbye
God   for instance   what
could that possibly mean anymore?
or Garbage
The word floats
free of the smells and the flies
the oil spills   dead
birds
It reconnects
with its old French roots
Garb-a-a-aaje-uh
Classy   really
designer garbage
garbage god
I had wanted to write
about singing on my bike
through the early morning Berkeley streets
plum blossoms opening
cats catting   dogs dogging
most people still asleep
insulated dreaming souls
I had wanted to write about
what it felt like to love her
the slow way she moved
thigh on thigh
how her snowy face would change
frowning almost

suffused with passion
But   Passion   Innocence
the words are exhausted
sliding in History's transparent gut
Language is speaking us
so many kids
flapping in grandfather's clothes
so many needles
in so many grooves
Then how come it feels so thin and
echoless
scribbling here?
Scared words in my head
yearning to enter
into yours
The page is a mortal space
as the world is a mortal space
It's an opaque white bridge
like a synapse
and each poet
that sets foot on it
is dying to get across

PERFECT STEALTH

There isn't any boy there
Patterns of light and dark
tiny dots
There was a boy
the light bounced off
squatting on his haunches
looking up at the camera
guarded?   wondering?
affronted by this
paunchy snapshooting
suitor of his grandma?
He was hunting pigeons
in the concrete triangular park
breakwater
  for the Broadway traffic
on this sheltered curving street
stalking the sleek
fat scuttling shapes
iridescent cloudy
trying to catch them with
perfect stealth
of Uncas   Natty Bumppo
Quarry all around
      pigeons
jungle traffic
Trying to catch them
as the picture catches time
that boy
old men and women
sunning in the bouncing light

DOOR

The words blackened
swarmed senselessly as ants
Something tremendous sailed
off the edge of my brain
Disappearance
an active principle
flashed like a sign
Disappearance
like a wall where a door used to be

The next day I remembered
or thought that I did
drinking Aunt Dorothy's perfume
I must be three or four
and I lie on her bed
in her ruffled scented bedroom
I'm drunk
and twisted voluptuously
enslaved

I remembered being older
seven   or eight
in the long hall of our Washington Heights
    apartment
Aunt Dorothy is in the bathroom
and I'm trying to see through the keyhole
and I can't
How to say the fire of her imagined body?
I'm filled with hopeless rage
    at the door   at the blocked keyhole

I think I sneaked and kept silent
but I have a trace memory
that I roared and pounded at the door
and she laughed

I'm in my late teens
dressed in tie and jacket
and I'm dancing with Dorothy
at some family function
She's in her mid-fifties
and she's dying of cancer
I'm embarrassed that she's asked me to dance
that she holds me pressed tight
pressed against her actual
cancerous breasts and belly
She stares into my eyes
with hers   great   green
shining   seeming to whirl on themselves
"I've always loved you, Richard," did she say?
"I see an enormous sadness in you."
Now   writing this
Dorothy's body is clouds
She's been dead more than thirty years
Disappearance is flashing
and my words are black
as if they   themselves
are blocking my view
Is her death the door?
I don't know
I don't know
if there's any connection at all

THE HORSES

The actual ride was thrilling enough
generic triumph of it
horseback through redwood forests
galloping on hills overlooking
the sea
left eyelid scratched by branches
an ischial callosity pounded raw
sore
on the strange insides of my thighs
And when I got home from Camp Meeker
my mother's letter was waiting for me
telling of Mac's death
how he had called the day before
to inquire after Pop
said he wasn't feeling
so well himself
a "bubble" he couldn't
get rid of
how his girlfriend Barbara
had entered his apartment
after unanswered telephone messages
found him sitting on the toilet
in his pajamas
The two events tangled together
Mac rose like some
bottom fish in the shining
an exultation at first
even his dying
an end   a shape
Uncle Mac   the family schlemiel

unsinkably dimwitted
his spark of joy   nasal
rumbling
But there was a muddy suck
in Mac's death
narrowness   an anger
Months later
visiting my parents in New York
Cousin Joey came to dinner
I saw him after twenty years

At the time of the ride
and the death
at my mother's stern request
I had written to Mac's sons
Howard and Joey
round phrases to neglected family
bright veins in a darkness
Now here was Joey
fat   bald   graying
sweet and broken as a hamster
Joey looked like Mac
but slighter   still boyish
something massive in Mac's
old man's sloping
his head   belly   the nubbing
of his knees
And Mac had looked like Grandpa Joseph
but thickened   homely
without the arrowed serenity

slim   dark   handsome   of his father
    Collapsing cups
Joseph   Mac   and Joey
Joseph's namesake
I met Joey in the foyer
embraced him   He was very
emotional   asked me
about myself   and I gave him
some quick details   ended by saying
"I love my life"   Half true
More than half   but I omitted
the poverty   the desperation
Joey seized on my words   over-
reacted   not enviously   so much
as with hunger   And then he talked
talked about himself   His mother
Mac's beloved Ruth   had died in
birthing him   and Joey was brought up
by his grandfather   Ruth's father
Mac off selling on the road   His grandfather
Joey said   was the only one
who loved him
and when he died   Joey was sent off
to school   He was several times
in private hospitals   for depression
always voluntarily   and then
in a disturbed debt-ridden time
after the breakup of Joey's marriage
Mac had committed him
to a locked ward   violent ward

of Manhattan State Public Hospital
After that experience   and the legal struggle to
free himself   Mac   Joey said
became a terror to him   Long separation
And when he saw his father again
even after many years   it was with a certain
uncontrolled trembling

Revelation   like the turning
of a gem   I had never thought of Mac
as a terror to anybody   Dark Mac
the punisher   And oddly
as Mac changed in my mind
my memory of the horseback ride
changed too
I remembered the brute intractable
head of Dusty
    my slow safe mare
pale yellowish eyes like marbles
How big she was   brown and gray
round sleek horseness of her
how hard to set in motion
stubborn and heavy-limbed
My friends had warned me
to be firm
she might rebel   act up
to be careful currying her
never to get myself in position
to be kicked or stepped on
So there was a verge

of menace in Dusty
her size
animal silence
I remembered moments
galloping
when my feet had slipped deep
in the stirrups
and I felt myself pitched forward
off balance   too high on her withers
no real fear
but something in me had
entertained falling
almost acquiesced
Even the landscape
when we broke from the flickering
of the forest
those raw golden hills
shaggy   sundrenched
the sea several miles below
covered with low cloud
seemed remote in the glare
alien
The memory ride became a
journey into a void
the animals   the earth
a dispossession

Some enormous longing
Transcending on my bumpy butt
the horses the engines

As if I could leap up and grab
something   hold on
just by wanting it   and
naming it
But what?
And what did that Northern California
paradise have to do with Mac
his narrow-skied East coast
grit and sorrow?
Not that Mac had been sad
He had a gift for pleasure
But his life surely
had been hard
He had lost Ruth   his first
love   delicate   tubercular
in childbirth
His second wife   Bert
Howard's mother   had died of cancer
And yet a third wife   Edith
that tiny-minded *yentah*
but he had cared for her
had died a few years before
in the aftermath of bypass surgery

It oppressed me
Mac   I realized
had always oppressed me
since my childhood
the way his eyes would twinkle
bantering   to cross swords

with my brightness
to draw me into an
airless muddy-minded debate
about religion or school pride
tastelessness of the dry kosher meat
provincialism of his life in Paterson
with Bert and Howard
All Mac's years on the road
selling Niagara vibrators   and later
when he grew older
out of a store in Hoboken
the blinkered tenacity of it
sloping sagging knuckliness of it
Christ   it was like being drawn
doubled and gasping
through some dark vein of kitsch
in urban rock
Irksome harness
as when a child
I was pulled from my sultan's play
to visit the family
these common boring people
linked to me only
by birth   by blood
Mac was sucking the ride
down to schlemieldom
How ridiculous my
leap out of poverty
hunger for
the animal   the elemental

Mac superposed upon everything
as if I roiled in his sullenness
his resentments
trotted ranges
of his sloping belly
nubbled knees
of his liver and guts
And at the center
straight   flamelike
stood Grandpa Joseph
who had died young
when my mother was four
when Mac was eight or nine
who had left behind an aura
of gentility   of poetry
Joseph   leader
of their Romanian immigrant community
arbiter   the beacon
But I had heard Mac
grumble about his father
when my mother invited him to dinner
two years before
He had seemed obscurely on trial
as if my mother were a witness
and I some kind of judge
"He couldn't even make a living,"
he said fixedly,   "He was
a conductor on the trolley . . .
he tried to sell insurance—
you remember, Helene!"

of course my mother remembered almost
nothing of that time
and made the nurturing excuse
that Joseph had already been sick
But after Mac left
she told me again
about his resentment of his father
how Mac had always
felt slighted
because he was the slow one
Joseph thought him
stupid
how even when they walked on the street
Joseph spotless   beautifully dressed
Mac had always dwelt   she said
upon the beauty of his father's clothes
Joseph walked ahead
always a pace or two ahead
as if he were ashamed of Mac
as if he were trying
before the eyes of the community
to disown him
Listening to my mother
I had a sudden comprehension
of Mac's doubt
that first crumbling
that drove him
the courses that he took
when his children were grown
all that doggish activity

of course Mac
was naturally vital   doggish
but the Jewish History
Psychology   the Literature
samba   tennis lessons
As if he were proving himself
his style   worth
as if he were running
from the back of his own head

Joey swam back to me
forlorn boy in the gray
paunchy man
still sensitive   slender inside
the boy who had never known
his mother
who bore the unspoken
blame for her death
He was trying so hard to stay out
of the hospital
to become human
talking in jokes
in hip wiseguy
desperation
his son   his daughter
staying off drugs
therapy groups
weight-watcher's groups
And Mac his father
who had spent his life

trying to catch up
to his own father
to pull even
thick   twinkling
in the pastures of manly respect
I saw
a fiery ring
of fathers and sons
wrongs   resentments   thwarted
love
and beyond   barely sensed
the molten
sea of souls
terrible depth   resonance
Suddenly I felt myself
a limb of my family
no matter how I stretched and leaped
anxious green twig
twisting out to the Pacific
I pulled the pictures
Mac had snapped
out of the envelope
my mother had sent them in
"for you to remember us"
True to his Macness
he had beheaded me and my father
in two of the three pictures
at the foreheads   at the neck
But in the good one
there we are

the three of us
my mother between
our arms around her
standing against the living room drapes
"We all look
a little older than our mental images"
my mother had written
Her lips are pursed for the camera
in her sexy
rhumba music pose
my father
in his old man's semi-crouch
suavely   dutifully smiling
Ironically the snapshots become
my remembrance of Mac
That visit was the last time
I saw him alive
the bantering gone
beaming and courteous
and oddly humble
like a peasant bowing
down to a prince
As if he knew
Mac was making his arrangements
that brittle rapprochement with Joey
and   incredibly
his bar mitzvah
that he studied for   gave to himself
at the age of seventy-six
Looking at Mac's photos

I feel everything dissolving
my mother and father
wrinkling   melting
my own flesh
sinking on my bones
It's like swinging into a gallop
the way the horse seems
to falter
to fall down to its gait
and then you're galloping
fleet
as if burning in time
heavenly horses
nothing to hold to
no way to rein in

And this is where the poem
pulls apart
The dream ride
It wants
to be a ceremony   a prayer
It wants to realize
that tree of blood
our family
one trunk
with branches stretching
across a continent
to give a dead man
who wouldn't have wanted it
who would have preferred

Fisherman's Wharf   or Disneyland
the tawny power of the hills
the horses   of that great sighing space
that isn't mine to give
anyway
city man   garret poor poet
Release is what the poem wants
to unite Mac with the horses
to make Joey love himself
to free me   myself
from my own anxious cycling
And how   of course
can these words do that?

I did go riding again though
in the spring
The deep forested gullies
were lush
The restless waving grasses
of the hills were greener
I had a different horse too
Apache
a small spirited gelding
who wanted to lead
to run
We didn't see the Pacific this time
the day was warm and hazy
or the Russian River
in its tight green valley
nosing to the sea

But from time to time
I thought of Mac
and of Joey
when I wasn't thinking
of controlling Apache
or of how the saddle
was pounding my butt
again and again on the same sore spot
and I imagined
that I was riding Kaddish for him
for Uncle Mac
that I was riding
for what was missed

STEPPING OVER THE ROOFPOLE

You are just your own
angry festooned little cabin
spine and roofpole one
creaking of mortality
Still tilling this invaluable red acre
of your flesh
What else to plow
but these lumpy fields?
    It's midnight
on the bone farm
   The words step on ahead
out of the circle of firelight
into the forest
where poems grow
like gillyflowers behind the leaves
pale blue faces
of old dead men

INKLINGS

I

My father wasn't driving.
I sat in the front seat. We got lost
and made a U-turn in a driveway. The car tilted
as we turned. Feeling of magical efficacy,
the gear shift in the floor,
packed groin fruit of the dashboard.
Back on the right road we drive towards a green mountain,
drive and drive. The mountain floats pale as emerald
against the blue sky, always in the distance,
never nearer.

II

Pop and I are pissing together, laughing,
making the Yellow Cross. His hairy body, his huge penis,
streaming. Like a neck and a face, like some mute
awed creature.

III

My father's office, 1650 Broadway,
gazing across his desk out of the window. Swirl
of steam above the black tarpaper roof of a theatre,
the marquee, traffic and people. A sense of deep
twinings, of the city's countless plots and despairs.
Like moles swimming in a field underground.
A world of hidden moving powers.

SCRYING SOUL

When my mother arranged these pictures
more than forty years ago she did it hopefully
joyously   as a bird makes its nest
our row of photos along the top
of the spinet piano clock paintings

the tutelary spirits
that used to be a lamp

He plays the violin bowed sash bows on his shoes
She sings holding the score
Their heads angle together bodies swayed
blown to music

so that these pictures
my mother and father on each end
her parents Granma Grandpa Joseph
me triune two baby snaps pressed into the frame
the six-year old me sitting my thought ladder
before our old window on Broadway

seem suspended in a geyser
of silent music

It's our family shrine

Splayed here on the couch on my trips back
I look at it
scrying my life reading my entrails

When the weather in New York drops below thirty
    you can hear the clock's sharp ticking

It looks like a head and the paintings
            Stanley's oil of a vase
      the two imitation oils
    man and woman again   Japanese? Italian?
      Romantic in dashed
        faux impressionist strokes

    are like wings
      flying the piano in its wall of sky

THE TEST

All night long the dragons roared
hunting in the tunnels
to lay their glowing eggs
All night long in the Underworld
where the separate heads and houses came together
where the goggle engineer with a light on his helmet
was sliced like cheese
and they carried his mortal lumps under canvas
up the steps in the sunlight by the Rexall Drug Store
from the black monster trains

Sometimes
when I got off at my stop
I stood alone
while the other passengers hurried away
my body squeezed between the pillar and the cars

slowly it started
then faster and faster
thundering
light deathroaring by
Squeezed motionless in terror
for a moment I entered
the fire belly of the city

then slamming by
a dizzy suck of void
it shrank down the track
lights
red   yellow   green
the tunnels branching like questions

DRAGONSCAPE

The angel police   screamed round Palazzo Oedipal
      world crack
Broadway inscribed   scarring in two
      white and black
Dragon was the subway

  That was momentous terrain

    great jumbling bodies   curving down to the river

always fires on under the mountain
   scream wheels turning

    No people
     You see it's a
magical beast machine all the power words together

COMING BACK

There had crouched trying to name it now
  a complex shaggy beast whose spine was Broadway
or the subway glowing beneath jumble city
   and that afternoon in the still August sun   more
    than forty years later I felt it rise
     shamble off

    I was looking out across the Hudson
where my father had lifted me up over the railing
   to sun dazzle   ships on the river
    The belly of space

    The Jersey shore ranked thick
with new buildings and our old neighborhood
  for long gone rich men at the other end
of the century   plazas curving drives
    had become Dominican   Broadway
   shrunken telephoto march
    of black and brown shoppers
     shimmering bodegas

    Time is a belly too
I had left my mother's small Queens apartment
  where time was eating us alive
  to   what? touch back to my childhood?
  rescue myself in that dragonscape?

    Sat on our stoop
     tranced
      in the doubleness

                   past
                   present
             strolled to the top of the street
               where the thighs of the buildings met
                 packed groin of overpass
                 railroad
                         pedestrian bridge
             Larry and I had hooted through
                 its echo tunnel
               muggy summer days like this
             to our dead dog   bottle and condom
               adventures on the river

           So new kept up! not crumbled or demolished
                 this fenced oval park and plaza
           where I'd skated   where the older boys
                 played roller hockey
           And still   I only realize the stillness now
                 Where were the kids?
             Hardly a soul on the street   a few
                 gazers   couples
                       on Riverside Drive
             Who lived in these apartments now
                 off the Spanish Broadway hustle
           in these massive fortresslike buildings
                     with their sunglittered windows?

                   She was the only one I saw
             queen bee of the solitude
                 a beautiful young Latina

reading on the stairs in an entrance court
         dark curly brown hair
            full fruity mouth
Soundboothed in a frown of concentration
      she held the book close to her face
            Not a flicker my way
         She read me out

      I wanted to approach her
         to enter her kept air
            I wanted I began to burn

      But what would she have seen?
      An ecstatic balding older man
            in a striped tee shirt
         And what would I have said
I was a kid here
         half a century ago
            and I want to make love to you?

      Still   on my circuit back off the river
I glanced in at her ogled hopelessly
         and went on counting the places
      heroics terrors
A car rolled by
         only other sign of life
         sitting low on its shocks
            blaring salsa music
Washington Heights I had read
         became the center of Dominican crack trade

So did the dealers live here posh lower Heights
in these silent carefully tended buildings?
my lovely Latina some drug lord's
mistress?

And as I turned the corner of our old block
it hit me Goneness
as if a starfish had everted its stomach
sucked the streets and houses
to a clean stone socket

Ghost of goneness
toiling up the block in that heat
the familiar yellow building
floated in the notch at the top
tilted across Broadway at the angle of ascent
It had been a savings bank
those years ago out our living room window

Like toiling up the birth canal
Time the laundry scent rising
off my dead father's shirt
a mango-mouthed woman
jalopy rolling on Latin music

When I sat back down on the stoop
600 West 157th Street
it was like a museum or a stage set
drug rehab where the cleaner's used to be
two black jivers laugh-calling to a third

I'd sat here in leaden terror
           waiting to fight Sanford
      I'd watched that little man
           totter the pavement   fall
              smashed glasses blood orbits
      there across the street
           in front of the kindergarten
      Not then but now
my mother's eyes spread vast across the windows
           eyes of a sharper
                deeper leaving

      Went out front sat in the pigeon park
      in the power stream
           Black working men on the benches
      where my Granma had sunned flirted
              with her elderly suitors
         this triangular concrete park
like a breakwater against the Broadway traffic
         our apartment house smiling behind
         on its sheltered curving street
   Counted up   fifth floor
      Those were our windows
         That's where we lived

   When I looked back down my gaze locked
with a handsome fortyish Black man
      sitting on a bench across from me
         "What's he grinning about?"
   was he thinking? or did he figure he knew?

Wait waver
then he gave me an almost
        imperceptible nod
And we were gone
        as if we'd never existed
        that family   my childhood
            an odd bittersweet dream
melting behind this new wave of people
bright day glo colored shops
        NIGHT CLUB *zapateria*
        and behind that a hum a
            streaming

I sat there
        some ten fifteen minutes
burning in details
        but eased
            given over to emptiness

Then I went down the subway steps
        and took the train
back to the junior-four apartment in Queens
    where my mother was finishing her lunch
        where we were merely real
            she and I
            and really dying

CRYING

I cried for my father
for his slim muscled legs
because he was too timid and shy
    for death
I cried for my childhood
my bedroom mouse
our long hall   apemen
    and dinosaurs   marching in the darkness
for Bach's climbing violins
ache of their beauty
too tangled in this world
to ever get out
for women
faces in sunlight
the places they were
songs that played
all those filaments of soul
itching under time's rock
The crying so deep
    it was like coming
bitter crying
crying sweet like milk

FLYING

It bolted onto the windowsill
its dials for speed
and fuel
its steering wheel
that pushed in pulled out
to dive or climb

He flew into the aircourt
sun exploding reflected
in the windows
brick walls
small sky at the top

body of the years
in that flight
body of the dreams
inside that house
Madeleine of the roseate
nipples Blackie
the Polish butchers

the flight transparent
flowering flame
World War II tracers
Korean dogfights
He dove down aching
into death
climbed back out
bigger   stronger

Superimposed upon the aircourt
body of the building
leavened window bread
of lives that lived
inside it
rising body
of those many lives

He understood nothing about time
the twisted knuckly hands
about money
the main chance
about baby cries
answerless walls
in which death was breathing

Each single life
without alternative
Silvia of the tickling
Mr. O'Riley
Melvin Cohen   two punches to the head

These bled back to him later   invisible fuselage
body of the plane
flying towards your body, reader
the city of your body   flying unwritten inside

NEW POEMS

LENOX HILL HOSPITAL

"We apologize" voice on the phone
"but your mother has expired."
Ex-spired breathed out her soul
Saw her dying like a dormouse against a slab
of sky
spired pyred crashed and burned tired deep
"Please listen . . . She didn't suffer . . . slipped
into a coma . . ." awkward and earnest
working to be kind his speech mired
in a thick accent from the city where I was
born New York subways deli's clubs
check-cashing emporiums
its miles and miles of motherless street

TANTRUM

Death is the mother of beauty
My mother is dead But I'm not
beautiful

Do you follow
my reasoning? my
faux-naif conundrums? how
I eat at the world with words

Throwing a death tantrum

which is to gnaw at emptiness

which is to chew on stillness

1954

You could roll that coin
aways Light up your leaving home pinball machine
Larry and me sitting down by the rocks
a freighter sharp in the distance toylike
cleaving slowly past us down the middle
of the river

DOG'S EYE

We'd wandered farther up the river
than ever before up past the bridge
to a broad curve a swale Families
were picnicking Grande Jatte by the
Hudson we noodling slouching past
down towards the water
where it sucks at the rocks when we
found the dead dog

carnival of its death tar
nival slick black grin

It lay on its side in a mudpit
noseless fat pigdog
Savage fetor
when it caught the wind as we
circled it sharp crawling smell

Larry threw a rock *thud*
high whickering laugh
obscene because it scared him
thud   *thud*
I saw the flesh quiver

So I yelled stopped him shoved him

felt sorry for its death its
stench and dignity jaws drinking the mud

see it spreading longshot George
Washington Bridge

spooky death of my childhood
banana split death of the horror
comic books dignity dognity
syzygy

Moving

Swollen with lasttimeness
as I have been all my life
I told him I'd take trains back
we could still go down to the river

Larry was quiet didn't buy it

It seemed to me a golden thing we did
our rambles by the Hudson past the playground
to the Bridge beyond
rats gulls condoms barges

In my memory
we're tiny as fleas Larry and me on that
mystic body by that wide
silvery cloaca

I'm blurring him over Larry Lucas
thin towheaded kid
loner snickerer getaway guy

I remember once he taunted Johnny
his me too showoff noisy little brother
got him flexing straining his skinny arms
to pop cannonballs
Then he pulled down Johnny's shorts

Once wrestling in my room on my bed
I pinned him started to tickle him
felt his whippiness and a strange excitement

flushed through imagining Madeline
his mean pinched sexy older sister
in her parochial school uniform
short skirt kneesocks bucking underneath me

Larry's mother was dying
cirrhosed her yellow skullhead
too heavy for her neck

We never said a word about her

Or his father that he looked just like
as if they were time's double Mr, Lucas
a furious speechless Larry thickened
drooping in the eyelids moustaches

We did our things together
balance-walking
on the old green patina cannons
in the courtyard of the Indian Museum
strolling over the hump of Broadway
to the Dumars Theater at 145th St.
our river trip that long block
to the underpass as if slipping
inside a fissure of the city
wooden walkway over the tracks
and down to the water

Riverside Drive strip of green
that runs the whole west flank of Manhattan

wide power flow ships tour boats
We did the playground hunted on the rocks
hiked farther and farther up the shore
But when I think of that riverine world
I remember best just sitting   professing
books that I read the insides
of the body anatomy physiology
It seemed to spark us talking science
Sun a star stars plasmas where atoms are made
felt generous to draw that seething
of creatures for him
trilobite allosaurus smilodon
against the New Jersey shore

I did take the train back
to Washington Heights once
but not for forty years

And the way we actually parted
Larry spun and punched me "Gotya last!"
he crowed and ran up the stairs
me huffing after popeyed
I knew I'd never catch him
Got to his door just as he slammed it
in my face stood there incredulous
boggled hearing him slide down
the inside shrieking with laughter

PARADIGM

i

I was riding the F train
senior year of high school
bursting from the tunnel
into Fifth Avenue Station
when I saw the dark train light up
felt like God because I knew
Everything has a cause a set
of causes right? in given conditions
only one thing can happen
yes? the way billiard balls
can only click and go
each moment rides rails
on the next Determinism obvious
but solid as a Christmas tree

Laplace on a train
in the twentieth century

ii

It was Leubie who blew out
my determinism to quanta
Heisenberg uncertainty sad Leubie
petname for my liver-lipped friend
Leubenthal

Among us supersmart he was the brain
head floating on his

vestige body like an octopus head
asway in ocean currents

spookiness of the ultra-small
what Leubie spoke to me
that one live week of friendship
roommates freshman year of college

conceiving in numb rapture
sparking far from any feeling

I argued that the world made sense
cause and effect
I argued that the subatomic
was a subset of the world machine
But my arguments dissolved that week
Cosmic chortling

His memory flits electronlike
professor of Physics at forty In therapy
to express his anger to his mother
He had a wife Kathleen who looked
like him female of his own heady
species but she was demanding
an open marriage
with her lesbian lover

Leubie
scared and gray
first man I knew alive on Prozac

Our week though he was an oracle
      dissolving mind in light
   like what I later saw on Acid
         sardonic white
      first beam of the sixties

ETERNITY

Pi-day take it out a few thousand decimals
pi-day   3/14   my birthday
rolling through the years
It's also Albert Einstein's birthday
That's always been key for me
and right near Jack Kerouac at 3/12
But this kid mild Asperger's
mathematical savant
sees it as pi a number
that approaches itself
as an asymptote
gets longer and longer
and so touches eternity
infinitesimally

HUB

The dream said
Ascension   Assumption   Grace &
Wheel Then as they tend
to do it vanished
A honeyhead dream clearly
b/ reaching distances
in its wheeling
cloud hub
rubbing up
and out

GODFIGHTER

When I was four I had my first idea
four when memory flowers   I
can't remember saying "I'm three"
but I said "four and a half" it seemed
for eons to various of Granma's
ingratiating suitors

My idea was this:
I'm a person too just like these people
I see around me Tremendous conception
It made sweet sense of the
raw tumbling phenomena Not just
a fountain of thusness from then on
I was me

bent on conceiving obsessed
(abscessed) with truth

Because clearly the person I was
was very very special

and truth was not my mother's
'telling the truth'
although I believed in that but
the twang in another dimension
God's eye

Curling back into that plasma
now that my mother is dead
and God's eye sees through me

that fascination of me-ness

I looked at my asshole in a mirror
tried to see up inside

thought
about my soul how lucky it was
amazing that my soul
was in me and not in Mr. Lucas
our super in a doorknob a cockroach

I tried to fit the interior
this momentousness I felt inside
with the outside my body
with other bodies my life
with other lives

Strange and shameful

my smells my chubby
body with its small tender
limbs

When I looked in a mirror
my eyes stood still
I thought I had weird frozen
eyes

But I also felt enormous

At the age of six I stopped
believing in God
Nay-sayer
my mind rose up like a fist

I loved muscles and teeth
everything wild and fierce
Animal over vegetable bees
over wasps Indians over
cowboys bulls over bullfighters

I was a Godfighter
fought God in the name of truth
And truth had begun its morph
from God's nonexistent eye
to Science

There was the power
Paleontology seething the oceans
crawling the land with glyptodons
and stegosaurs anatomy physiology
astronomy

Avid for its arguments and its terms
I brandished them memorized and deployed
them like artillery

So at the beginning
this new person I was turned
warrior and thief of the flame

HELENE

Grief repeats   repeats   scurries the past
a warren   lit underground
pops up facing her   long childhood hall
"What have you got in your hands, Richard?"

Little boy   looking up
as I look up now   that she's dead

Open my fists   full of Granma's pennies
right for me   left for Sanford
And she gives me the truth slap   the
honor slap   burning down

All the twists of our life converge
there   *intortocheat* each instant
until the end   angry birth   division
the eyes of my soul   "I'll always
be with you, Richard"

She said that   late in our life
after Pop had died   to ease
my dread of her death   said it
with love   arching conviction

But it's not so   There's silence
inside me   Mother of truth
mother of courage
That flesh woman is gone
alien   unknown
Only her echo   palm
of her hand scalding my cheek

ÎNTORTOCHEAT

Romanian word 'twisted' 'intricate' Language
of my mother's father   that I taught myself
to translate his poems   So it spirals out of itself
Grandfather Joseph   to my mother   to me   and from me
back towards the clear-eyed   unknowable void   of him
Like the shell of a nautilus   *a toarce* 'to spin'
a se intoarce 'to return'   But the *'ocheat'*
'eyed'?   as *ochi* 'eye'   *ocheada* 'glance'
So 'nautilus-eyed'?   'orb-spun'?   'twist-sighted'?

DEMENTIA

Transcendental puns   anagrams
how do they jive with
impossible love?   flower   wolfer
flow-er   I could only love her again
after she'd lost her mind
eyes   in bony outlines   flowering

What I Said

Woke up last night at 4:00   sliding down the pipe
to my death   dark red   jittery slide
the sump of metaphysics there
carnivorous   hoodoo
and like any baby monkey
on its wire frame
my soul turned to her
Late in her life   my mother took to calling 911
wee hour ambulance to the hospital
It was never dire   her eternal
stomach and intestinal ailments   Once on the phone
I even lectured her on the cost
of medical care   "It gets a little
scary, Richard   Can you understand that?"
I did I do   and when I sheepishly said so
we had a rare sweet moment of unity
That was fifteen years ago   "I love you, Ma
Don't be scared"   I said last night
mothering my dead mother   mothering my death
and then I went back to sleep

CHILDHOOD

I didn't want to kill my father   or
fuck my mother   I just wanted godhead
X-ray vision   chocolate milk shakes
I wanted to munch in the jungle
of my mother's eyes   as the tigers
spun to butter around Black Sambo's tree
It was the base   the baby tone   of paradise
It was all about me

my
concentric blooming   the me that shone
and showed the way   beacon   beconstruction
too busy a bee to de-

But I leap fifty years into theory
(Kill the author?   Fuck her?)

still on the be side
against the be-cide of the text

still a me-taphysician
although my me has filled up
with time and space
my me has multiplied

When my mother died
it flipped me back to childhood
Her eyes became the gateways to the stars

It was cold and gone out there
so I wanted to swim back to
the start

my mother's heart

I sank in
along the anfractuous sublime
to   (Here we are!)

Soul-ipsism
all the bees of me's
the I's of yous
hiving
in this honeycomb
of the poem

PILLOW

Touch of the pillow on my cheek
and when I rolled over
I could still feel it   whisper
of the feeling   like a small creature
dying   for which I had tenderness
and pity   and so I huddled my senses
to keep that touch alive   feel it   feel it
At the age of four   I wanted to preserve things
to save them   I was a stillness artist
listening into their absence   negative
times negative   became positive
those tender touches blooming in my blood

ELF POWER

I sit at the kitchen table   drubbing my mother
with Silbergian laws   Big yellow kitchen
with two separate entrances   curled
at the end of the hall   like the sun of the apartment
Silbergian Law #68:   How to eat chicken noodle soup:
slurp out the soup   put ketchup on the noodles
Silbergian Law #83:   Never mix leftover tomato soup
with leftover bean soup   My ukases are jokey
but fanatic   and my mother bustles under them
As long as I don't actually misbehave   I'm
her pantocratic little brain boy

On safari through my mashed potatoes
I'm advancing on my juicy hamburger
Silbergian Law #3:   Save the best for last
I'm conquering my lunch   bellowing
Silbergian Law #14:   All lunches end
in chocolate pudding

Kitchen-table-centric
Granma's two faces
Shuffling in in the mornings
without her false teeth   collapsed
hollow-cheeked   goggling like the clock
on the wall   My proud sweet-faced
rest of the day Granma
preparing her eggplant   and mamaliga
charming her suitors in the park
with her round rouged cheeks
Daddy grinning home from work

smelling like cigarettes and snow
We come joking and jerking down the hall
pressing magic buttons in to dinner
where we swim around the table   each
in his own plate
Silbergian Law #2: The supreme meal
is spaghetti   but also baked beans

Kitchen-table-ec-centric
Fleering over my shoulder
to the aircourt window   centri-fugal
It's elf power   God and Santa
consubstantial   "Who always knows"
I'm blending with the elfin   turbulent
gray   like wind with eyes   beginning to formulate
Silbergian Law #1:

THE BREAST

I was standing by my mother's bed
five years old   so we were almost eye to eye
No thoughts that I remember   I just reached out
and touched her breast   To my astonishment
my hand sank right in   I thought they'd
be hard and pointy   like torpedo tips
brassiere ads   "What are you doing, Richard?"
I looked up and our eyes met   She said it
very carefully

In our midnight myths
I bit her breast when I was born
because she couldn't give me milk
Huge between us in the darkness
bruised   hurting

Shame   I knew even then I'd done
something wrong   so I shrugged
looked away   My mother's careful silence
not to alarm me   I realize now   to disturb
the development of the starry man
she willed me to become   The incident passed
with a mild unease   But my thoughts
slid ahead   Rakish   peaked
that succulent bomb hung fire
Its astonishment lingered   almost airy
soft and fleshy

GUM WRAPPERS

I was a duke of the fourth grade ultra-smart kids
One lunch Leslie opened her mouth wide
and showed me her chewed-up raisins
Ugh! My fu man disgust act was so funny
her dark eyes sparked   she squealed with delight
and we fell in love

She chased me around class
and in the halls   declared her love
warm and flirtatious

Tough jolly duke I denied her
too bumptious   craggy and flame-browed
for love   But I did   I did
That was my secret

Alone in my room   Leslie shone blush light
tingling sweetness   I imagined myself
near her   across the city   on the doorman East Side
angel current in the motes and air
of her room   her doorknob   watching
and thrilling   Leslie Leslie   Anything
but myself   She was loving   loved
down to the mashed up glop in her mouth
And I was a wolf of shame

So I worked the erotics of no
before I knew what they were
kept myself safe   by acting amused

and coolly indifferent
while I lived for the transmogrified future
when I could save her   from drowning
from legions of tough kids in glorious fighting
and our love would declare itself
Wolf of denial   the tension was delicious
she and I   wound up and ticking   like a crimson clock

But Leslie declocked herself   after about a week
sadly and sweetly   She wanted the present
She wanted the erotics of yes   So our love
went underground   started to churn against itself
She had a club   the Kitcat Club   with Norma
and Irene   so I headed up the Anti-Kitcat Club
with Harvey and Neal   espionage
fake messages   I even pulled Norma's braids
at the bus stop   glared into her
wide gray eyes   The low came in sixth grade
when Leslie took up with the loathsome
Donnie Schulman   I punched him in the stomach
the old solar plexus trick   left him fishflopping
in the hall   But the crux had crinkled
long before   In fifth grade gym class
Leslie stepped forward   flanked by the Kitcats
and she held a silver ball   "I make this"
she announced   "Every day I add a gum wrapper
At the center is the name   of the one I love
with all my heart"   We sneered to each other
Neal Harvey and I   Of course the name at the

224

center was mine   But was it?   And the love
rolled away   wrapped in silver   entombed
empearled   growing farther and bigger

TONY

The size of his eyes   deerlike   lemur-
like   his body small and keen
he was a lepidopterist   a poet
an only child   like me   At thirteen
we crawled into an airshaft in the gym building
to get to the girls' locker room   Got
to the furnace room instead   where
we peeked at hairy Gale   the janitor
feeding it in flame light   Sex
was the driver   but also noGod
the thrill and inkling of death

His parents were Austrian Jews who
got out in time   They lived with Tony
in a foresty byway of Riverdale   the ritzy
west Bronx   a few blocks from our school
and I'd come there to sleep over   Strange
expression   as if I hovered over Tony's house
in sleep   His mother was a refined woman
dark and glittery   whose savory goulash
got even tangier on the second day for lunch
His father was an importer   a *gemütlich*
pipe-smoking man   warm and sly

On the night I'm thinking of we'd already eaten
were relaxing   preparing to split our separate ways
kids and parents   his father holding forth
waggish   slightly pompous   sounding us out
on art   his mother drifting   sleeveless dress
one arm draped behind the couch

226

when he turned suddenly   I see his finger
cocked   shaved hollow of her pale armpit
and he tickled her   I was amazed   She
jumped and shrieked   scolded him in German
But there was heat   I could feel she liked it

Upstairs in Tony's room   we started talking Freud
started to swim the unconscious   its Xness   its
Unness   We wanted to know what it knew
power source   wild   as a baboon's ass   as
the patterns on Tony's butterfly wings   punster
the dreammaker   From there we broached the queasy
question of sex with your mother   We rolled in that
like dogs   horror   titillation   disbelief   the ultimate
taboo   Boomlay boom   We drummed on it a while
Then   just before sleep   I found myself thinking
Of Tony's mother in a definitely new   a taboo way

Blackness   like suffocation   groping ahead
on and on   I was lost   alone   White fear
that the people had laughed and flashed
away while I slept   left me nowhere   no one
I wanted to moan   but something
closed my throat   groping ahead   that the blackness
would never end   fear   hell bright   like bio light
at the bottom of the ocean   "Silberg, what
the fuck are you doing?"   Tony   I'd been
sleepwalking   Tony pulled me back home
to the dark of his room

What was that about?   Sleepwalking?
Practically a zombie   a Frankenstein surged
by lightning   Next day   eating goulash   we tried
to dope it out   My family had moved   more than
a year before   from Washington Heights   where I
grew up   to Queens   that I hated   Could that be it?
that lostness   muffled terror?   Neither of us
much thought so   Tony sang on a message
a visceral wisdom   something more
than personal   liquid brown leaves of his eyes
I obsessed on his mother   Could she have played in?

to sex?   or death?   I never sleepwalked again
and our friendship tapered off through the years
of high school   to a hard bust up in college
but   but   I'm in blackness once more
high above the Hudson   in our old neighborhood
where my father and I used to stroll   A monument
there on Riverside Drive   a memorial plaque
for sailors in the First World War   unattended
forlorn   But now it's night   pressed   black
the plaque a stone door that won't let me through
to the city's monster flank   flame bowels   the dynamo

ACID

Pale blue cats   with bat faces
utter nonmeness
Mew   Mew   like the creak
of opening doors   Me   Mew   Me
Light
shone through the rosy fringes
of their ears   corpuscles   one by one
red microscopic crawl   Space
yawned   creaked wide
If those cats weren't me   who was?
Always   always   it was about godhead
But I saw no godhead in their eyes

ACID

A speck in space   shot through with space
wide screaming mouth where no sound
is heard   You could be swallowed   you could be
sucked away   How not   how not   Your killer mind
could stop the beating of your heart   Or
are you already dead   and wandered into Hell?
whose heart is fear   this new bright spiralling
fear   But is it new?   I can't remember
My senses a surface   rippling   and between
do I see shark maws?   Just tip
and you sink   slip sideways into depths
the cosmic gnash and crunch
No sound   no sound

Stay still   Stay absolutely still
trembling like a fawn   or rabbit
Feel yourself drain grey   with fear
that spirals up and up   so that it seems
your soul will snap   scream tight   and tighter
Then you remember   12 hours   Yes   You'll
be down in 12 hours   So you glare
at the clock   But the numbers just dance
They ring blind as a bell

WORKING IN FILMS

Tedious hours synching up the rushes
Allitalia   dental surgery films   test commercials
where I took the same light readings
for the model   and the shampoo bottle
Then I'd subway thunder home
to my room   the Yale Hotel   by Riverside Drive
flick on the light   and roaches fled
across the floor like wind through wheat
I'd eat my supper from some cans
and try to write

Exhaustion stained my mind   the mockers
I called them Bergman   Godard   Kurasawa
Everything that I was not   everything
my fists of flame could seize to be
Catch at the world with nervous nets
nervous nets   the willies

At the borders of sleep   that's when Ellen came
angled round across her shoulder
both mischievous and shy   bright eyes
my Swahili princess   I could feel her
slipping back across the waters
with spotlight steps

LOVE STAR

Only once I tried to rape a woman
Her face was scarred   tiger bit
let's say   She lived alone
in the East Village   That night my love star
had exploded   feeling empty
smashed up inside   Ciao   she said
smiling brightly down the subway stairs
So I rang tiger face's bell   She
buzzed me up   and I startes to press her
"C'mon   c'mon"   You're lucky   I thought
to get me   She stiffened   got
very quiet   and I grabbed her
shoved her back on the couch
started to yank up her skirt
"Don't   Please don't"   she began pleading
snarl face   her body clenched in a fetal
curve   white cotton underpants   mealy legs
I wilted then   of course   completely   wilted
"Sorry   sorry   sorry"   I said   till the silence
curdled   Then I split back to the night glow streets
trundling the ache   like a tank of dirty water
only then beginning to sense
how deep it was

THE ACHE

It was like the crumbling of a glacier
seeing her head   of a snake
of an orchid   "I think we're too different . . ."
over and over   over and over
And why did I love her when   because?   I
didn't want to fuck her   wing-shouldered
woman   lank and boyish   bright eyes
dilating and contracting like a butterfly
on its flower
As if she pixeled in from sisterland
where I dreamwalked   only child's
sisterland   sugary cleaving
That ache was astonishing
It stole my sleep
I was unbrothered
when she cleaved away

SPHINX

The wind plays the trees
   in Tomkins Square Park
like a xylophone   zippy and skeletal
hollow bone tones
Laissez les bone tones *roulez*

It's winter in the East Village
and I'm trying to survive
to burn on the updraft of all the heads
and join the larger ecstasy

But I feel she's swallowed me
and spit me out with something missing
   my gleam   the core of my apple

She seems to be getting
bigger and heavier   the wings
of her shoulders   sweep of her hair
curving down stony   vastly sphinxlike
in our wide private desert
Only her eyes   deeper maybe
live the same   That sidewise look
she gave me when she split
   bone tones   bone tones

So when I should be flashing

at the Peace Eye Bookstore   the Cinematheque
I catch instead at the corner of her eye
and fall like a tear

WIZARD

I broke down in Chomski's office
An elliptical orbit   revolving around two foci
Ellen   and Ellen   both suns
Voluptuous   almost   to go primal
down on hands and knees
in that room where he'd examined me as a child
to wallow   and sob
on the sound stage of childhood

Her eyes are the suns
Her mind is black space

I wanted Chomski to hear me
the way he listened when I was eight
and quoting *Gray's Anatomy*
He was my wizard then
Chomski the rumbler
showed me my bones on the fluoroscope
the shadow sack of my beating heart

Cracked now   cracked sack
I'd been taken with sobbing for two days
Walled up behind my subway face
I needed to cry

But Chomski barked
"Enough!   Stop!
A disease of sensitivity   You've got to be
        hospitalized

Six months   You'll get well
But you need to do this!"

Sudden white   a softness to that hospital
As if you could morph   vortex
          into its peace
It occurred to me
that sensitivity was a code word
for my family   my half mad
beautiful Aunt Dorothy   long dead
the overheated subset   of my mother and me
It occurred to me
there'd been some cosmic mistake
my mother and Ellen   each spinning in place
this older   smaller   grayer Dr. Chomski
"I don't need to go to any hospital"   I said
climbing dully up off his floor

He seemed to accept that   but he urged me
to see a psychiatrist   thrust the number at me
with a large shiny packet of Valium
"Use them, boychik   They'll calm you down"
I made polite noises   but I knew
I couldn't numb myself out
I had to yearn
I had to creep towards coherence
and the ache was all I had to go on

GLEAM

That Christmas rifle was
my favorite toy as play is prayer
as poetry is hunting

Its sliding bolt long barrel
penetrate the hollow of desire
zero power fire power

Playing at death

its obscenities contortions
dancelike throes

crack in my mind
split black
of my magic
brother rifle

I aim it at you

Our eyes meet
along that gleam

MEAT

He'd escape   spurt out of the rabbit cage
into our yard   with our chickens   two merino goats
I had to chase him down   tense and wiry
breathing fast   He'd freeze when I cornered him
He seemed to divine me standing above him
in the wraparound vision of his dark bulging eyes
Then   when I grabbed him   he'd rake my forearms
with his hind-legs   all the way back to the cage
A feral boy   he terrorized his cage-mate
a fluffy white rabbit half again his size
But I didn't kill him out of malice   I
killed him in dread   His mistress was planning
to make some rabbit fur gloves   "Let me do it"
I said   "I'm a carnivore   I need to know
the mystery of meat"   That's how I fell athwart
the mean white wire of his life   I studied
a pamphlet   Take his hind-legs in one hand
his head in the other   thumb between the ears
fingers curled under his chin   and snap him
like a branch   like cracking the breech of a gun
I set a day   I set a time   and I came to get him
reached in   he went into freeze mode
stroked him to calm him   as I got my grip
And I did it   I snapped him   but he didn't seem
to die   He convulsed   terribly   like gargling
I panicked   did it again   and again   and again

They skinned him   roasted him   stuffed with raisins
and wild rice   I took a ritual bite or two   tough
and chewy   but I had no appetite

Cloud rabbit   he comes back to me   broke-neck
goggle-eyed rabbit ghost   He's malevolent
but cold and blind   and his murder brings no wisdom

Camp Everett: Field Trip to a Dairy

The bull snorts   It sounds like a truck
We talking peanuts lined up outside his pen
I'd never been that close to a huge beast
before   trucklike sound   bull smell
Suddenly my guts fell out   Mortal terror
that this mountain of muscle
would crush me   Terror   like an electric
socket   I remember it across sixty years
Mithras created life   by capturing and killing
a sacred bull   Everything good and fruitful
sprang from its body   Black sun of bull's blood
They all kill the bull   the matadors   the butchers
to eat its great strength   pumped and stupid
to batten on its excess of life
          Raw beast of global black
it huffs above me   They're punching
and giggling   relaxed   They trust the bars
And I'm lit up in terror   sixty years away
In this poem the bull kills me   or looms to

FIRE

My mother came in the mail
like a review copy   tightly taped
in a cardboard box dense with her death
I've never opened it   I put her up
in my kitchen cabinet   by the wide
double windows   that look out on the garden
of Washington School   I'm not giving my mother back
to the water   to the ground   to the air
I keep her near me   her presence
in my life   Ma, there's a cherry plum tree
out my bedroom window   like nothing
in New York   It has a spike-haired look
from being lopped back to its nubs by the landlord
its twiggy sprouts of new branches   but in my eye corner
reading in the mornings   its red leaves
are a blood glory   It's the size of flight
Can you see it?   Can you hear the little boys
playing soccer on the school field?
"Score!   Score!   Sco-o-ore!" they jubilate
mimicking the TV announcers
That's how I dream to my longing   patient
tired momma   What?   ashes and bone char
there inside   my momma the lonely one
my momma the lioness
In the silence I build what we did
the long burn of our life
Only child   son of a frustrated Jewish mother
youngest daughter of a father who died
when you were just three   We were fated
to impossibility   to heartbreak

Ma, it stabs me   that I wasn't there
when you died   The sun comes up in my chest
remembering how we fell in love again
those last two years before   Washington School garden
is a fairy tale   overgrown   like Jack and the Beanstalk
Through the window you can see little kids
hiding from each other behind the hedges
trooping through and squatting down
to see the tomatoes   the chard   the flowers
Nothing much gets picked   Huge squash
and pumpkins crouch like mythic beasts
In tangled leaves   A spry little rat
runs up and down the fence post to the compost bin
Bees buzz   Hummingbirds gleam   We're out here
by the Pacific   across the vast country from New York
where both of us were born   We've come through fire   We're flying

STORING THE DAY

The squirrel scampers   start   stop   in the green plots
where the sidewalk meets the street   Its tail
ripples above it   like a dream it's having
Clear blue late fall day   light wind   I'm coming back
from shopping at the Berkeley Bowl   thinking
as I often do   about all the dead people I know
Lee   Sleazy Leesy   my old theater buddy
the countless auditions   the handful of shows
our pissing and parsing   Gielgud vs, Brando
Rorty vs. Plato   Suzanne   my former poetry student
who became my friend   who   before her suicide
seemed to be snubbing me   becoming   almost   my enemy
My mother   who lived so hard   My father   who lived
so softly   I feel them down beneath my feet
not so much underground   as kinetically down   flatlined
simplified   Overhead the sky mocks sublimely
slow vast revolving door   The squirrel cascades   here between
stiff little bucktoothed face   salt and pepper   merging to red
almost a fox color   on belly and tail   sparky calculus
of squirrelness   And I'm making like Rilke
saying "garden"   saying "tree"   "Bay Area"   "curve
of the Earth"   Still   as I walk through this flame-leafed day
those stopped shadows pull at me   Lee's eyes   depressed
acid   astonished   braggadocio   You fool, Lee
They saved you that first time it burst   put some weird
wire mesh in your stomach   But you went on eating
smoking   drinking   until that aortic aneurysm
burst again   got its sloppy seconds   Suzanne
Can't   Can't talk to you   even in memory   You're walled
You've severed yourself   just as you meant to do

in the shock waves of that gunshot   As if you felt hideous
ungainly   raw flesh   nerve endings   without a skin
as if the skin became   the beauty of your house and gardens
flawlessness of the dinner parties   Buddhism   philanthropy
therapy   poetry   But who could have imagined a bullet
in the brain   you whom violence so unstrung   that you'd do it
on the deck   for Bud to find you   A rage   revenge?   Or
delivering yourself   drilled baby   to his arms?   One time
One time only   says Rilke   and so I drink at this brilliance
bracketed between their deaths and my own   edges and
textures   this long-legged girl on her bike   perched rakishly
as she leans into her motion   these trees along the street
so distinctly leaved   colored   so much themselves   yet
like breathing   like smoke   The squirrel has flowed
up the stalk of a wilted sunflower   stopped
partway up   All I can see are his feet gripping it   bulk of
his body   eyes bulging at the sides of his head   odd suddenly
like a large bug   When my mother and father died
fourteen years apart   they became death central   My father
whom I loved so tenderly towards the end   reversed
like my child Daddy   who couldn't understand
why he wasn't in his TV chair   why he was in this
white place of constant needles and disturbance   My mother
who'd become demented   a wind wafting through her head
but still my mother   "The Boss" they called her at the home
lost and invincible   chattering in the dayroom   Fathomless
to store the beauty of this day against it   rehearsing   or
working my counter-magic   The big zeroing out
So simple actually   once you've seen it done   not
really strange   like other dimensions   strings   and so forth

The squirrel's tail is rippling   It's worked its way up
to the drooping flower   seems to have found some seeds
It nibbles and moves   short shifts   super-quick
Little dummy   pumping at the center of its life

Biographical Note

Richard Silberg is a poet, critic, translator, and associate editor of *Poetry Flash*. His poetry book *Deconstruction of the Blues* received the PEN Oakland-Josephine Miles Literary Award 2006 and was nominated for a Northern California Book Award. He is author of *Reading the Sphere: A Geography of Contemporary American Poetry*, essays, and several co-translations, among them *The Three Way Tavern*, by South Korean poet Ko Un, co-translated by Clare You, which won the 2007 Northern California Book Award, and *This Side of Time*, poems by Ko Un, White Pine Press, 2012.